PENGUIN CLASSICS

EARLY POEMS
A BOY'S WILL, NORTH OF BOSTON,
MOUNTAIN INTERVAL, AND OTHER POEMS

ROBERT LEE FROST was born in San Francisco, California, on March 26, 1874, and moved with his mother and sister to Lawrence, Massachusetts, in 1885. He attended Dartmouth College for less than a semester and Harvard College as a special student for two years. Working as a chicken farmer and as a teacher in Derry, New Hampshire, he wrote poetry at night. He and his wife, Elinor, moved their family to England in 1912, where his first two books, *A Boy's Will* and *North of Boston,* were published in 1913 and 1914. When Frost returned to the United States in 1915, he had become an important American poet. Over the next five decades, he published nine more volumes of poetry, and his reputation as one of the century's most powerful poets grew. In addition to teaching at Amherst, the University of Michigan, and Harvard, Frost received over forty honorary degrees and four Pulitzer Prizes. Frost read at John F. Kennedy's inauguration in 1961, the same year the U.S. State Department sent him on a "good-will mission" to Russia. Frost died in Boston, Massachusetts, January 29, 1963.

ROBERT FAGGEN is the Barton Evans and H. Andrea Neves Professor of Literature at Claremont McKenna College. He is the author of *Robert Frost and the Challenge of Darwin* and editor of the *Cambridge Companion to Robert Frost,* the *Selected Poems of Edwin Arlington Robinson,* and *Striving Towards Being: The Letters of Thomas Merton and Czeslaw Milosz.*

EARLY POEMS

ROBERT FROST

EDITED WITH AN
INTRODUCTION AND NOTES
BY ROBERT FAGGEN

PENGUIN BOOKS

PENGUIN BOOKS

Published by the Penguin Group

Penguin Group (USA) Inc., 375 Hudson Street, New York, New York 10014, U.S.A.
Penguin Group (Canada), 90 Eglinton Avenue East, Suite 700, Toronto,
Ontario, Canada M4P 2Y3 (a division of Pearson Penguin Canada Inc.)
Penguin Books Ltd, 80 Strand, London WC2R 0RL, England
Penguin Ireland, 25 St Stephen's Green, Dublin 2, Ireland (a division of Penguin Books Ltd)
Penguin Group (Australia), 250 Camberwell Road, Camberwell,
Victoria 3124, Australia (a division of Pearson Australia Group Pty Ltd)
Penguin Books India Pvt Ltd, 11 Community Centre,
Panchsheel Park, New Delhi – 110 017, India
Penguin Group (NZ), 67 Apollo Drive, Mairangi Bay, Auckland 1311,
New Zealand (a division of Pearson New Zealand Ltd)
Penguin Books (South Africa) (Pty) Ltd, 24 Sturdee Avenue, Rosebank,
Johannesburg 2196, South Africa

Penguin Books Ltd, Registered Offices:
80 Strand, London WC2R 0RL, England

This volume first published in Penguin Books 1998

13 15 17 19 20 18 16 14

Selection, introduction, and notes copyright © Robert Faggen, 1998
All rights reserved

LIBRARY OF CONGRESS CATALOGING IN PUBLICATION DATA
Frost, Robert, 1874–1963.
[Poems. Selections]
Early poems / Robert Frost; edited and with an introduction and
notes by Robert Faggen.
p.   cm.—(Penguin twentieth-century classics)
Includes bibliographical references (p.   ).
ISBN 978-0-14-118017-5
I. Faggen, Robert.   II. Title.   III. Series.
PS3511.R94A6   1998
811'.52—dc21   98–4324

Printed in the United States of America
Set in Bembo
Designed by Virginia Norey and Sabrina Bowers

CONTENTS

INTRODUCTION   xi
SUGGESTIONS FOR FURTHER READING   xli
A NOTE ON THE TEXTS   xliii

A BOY'S WILL

Into My Own   3
*The youth is persuaded that he will be rather more than less himself
for having forsworn the world.*
Ghost House   4
He is happy in society of his choosing.
My November Guest   6
He is in love with being misunderstood.
Love and a Question   7
*He is in doubt whether to admit real trouble to a place beside
the hearth with love.*
A Late Walk   9
He courts the autumnal mood.
Stars   10
There is no oversight of human affairs.
Storm Fear   11
He is afraid of his own isolation.
Wind and Window Flower   12
Out of the winter things he fashions a story of modern love.
To the Thawing Wind   14
He calls on change through the violence of the elements.

A Prayer in Spring   15
  *He discovers that the greatness of love lies not in forward-looking
  thoughts;*
Flower-Gathering   16
  nor yet in any spur it may be to ambition.
Rose Pogonias   17
  He is no dissenter from the ritualism of nature;
Asking for Roses   18
  nor from the ritualism of youth which is make-believe.
Waiting—Afield at Dusk   19
  He arrives at the turn of the year.
In a Vale   20
  Out of old longings he fashions a story.
A Dream Pang   21
  He is shown by a dream how really well it is with him.
In Neglect   22
  He is scornful of folk his scorn cannot reach.
The Vantage Point   23
  And again scornful, but there is no one hurt.
Mowing   24
  He takes up life simply with the small tasks.
Going for Water   25
Revelation   26
  *He resolves to become intelligible, at least to himself, since there is no
  help else;*
The Trial by Existence   27
  and to know definitely what he thinks about the soul;
In Equal Sacrifice   30
  about love;
The Tuft of Flowers   32
  about fellowship;
Spoils of the Dead   34
  about death;

Pan with Us 36
  about art (his own);
The Demiurge's Laugh 38
  about science.
Now Close the Windows 39
  It is time to make an end of speaking.
A Line-Storm Song 40
  It is the autumnal mood with a difference.
October 42
  He sees days slipping from him that were the best for what they were.
My Butterfly 43
  There are things that can never be the same.
Reluctance 45

NORTH OF BOSTON

The Pasture 49
Mending Wall 51
The Death of the Hired Man 53
The Mountain 60
A Hundred Collars 65
Home Burial 73
The Black Cottage 78
Blueberries 82
A Servant to Servants 86
After Apple-Picking 92
The Code 94
The Generations of Men 98
The Housekeeper 107
The Fear 117
The Self-Seeker 122
The Wood-Pile 132
Good Hours 134

MOUNTAIN INTERVAL

The Road Not Taken   137
Christmas Trees   138
An Old Man's Winter Night   141
A Patch of Old Snow   142
In the Home Stretch   143
The Telephone   152
Meeting and Passing   153
Hyla Brook   154
The Oven Bird   155
Bond and Free   156
Birches   157
Pea Brush   159
Putting in the Seed   160
A Time to Talk   161
The Cow in Apple Time   162
An Encounter   163
Range-Finding   164
The Hill Wife   165
   I Loneliness—Her Word   165
   II House Fear   165
   III The Smile—Her Word   166
   IV The Oft-Repeated Dream   166
   V The Impulse   167
The Bonfire   169
A Girl's Garden   173
The Exposed Nest   175
"Out, Out—"   177
Brown's Descent or the Willy-Nilly Slide   179
The Gum-Gatherer   182
The Line-Gang   184
The Vanishing Red   185

Snow   186
The Sound of the Trees   202

POEMS TO 1922
(Later published in *New Hampshire*)

A Star in a Stone-Boat   205
The Census-Taker   208
Maple   210
The Ax-Helve   217
The Grindstone   221
Paul's Wife   224
Wild Grapes   229
Place for a Third   233
Two Witches   236
  The Witch of Coös   236
  The Pauper Witch of Grafton   241
Fire and Ice   245
Dust of Snow   246
To E. T.   247
The Aim Was Song   248
For Once, Then, Something   249
Blue-Butterfly Day   250
The Onset   251
Good-by and Keep Cold   252
Not to Keep   253
A Brook in the City   254
Evening in a Sugar Orchard   255
The Valley's Singing Day   256
Misgiving   257
A Hillside Thaw   258
Plowmen   260

On a Tree Fallen Across the Road   261
The Lockless Door   262
The Need of Being Versed in Counry Things   263

EXPLANATORY NOTES   265
INDEX OF TITLES AND FIRST LINES   271

INTRODUCTION

In 1961, Robert Frost, overcoming old age and bad weather, recited his poem "The Gift Outright" to millions, becoming the first American poet to read at a presidential inauguration. A year later, President Kennedy asked Frost to act as a special ambassador to the Soviet Union and to deliver a message of "peaceful rivalry" to Premier Nikita Khrushchev, a considerable responsibility given the tensions of the time. Rarely in modern history had there been such a connection between poetry and power, a connection of a kind that rightly produces skepticism in critics and readers. Robert Frost had become the closest thing in the history of American letters to a national monument, a symbol of the Yankee virtues of independence, stoic belief, hard work, and common wisdom —in short, a sage. A color photograph of a white-maned and smiling Frost graced the March 1962 cover of *Life* magazine with the caption "America's Ageless Poet." His unprecedented and still unmatched four Pulitzer prizes, as well as forty-four honorary degrees, already had confirmed his place as the king of American poets. Frost enjoyed his fame but held a deeply ambivalent attitude toward his audience and its expectations. Cultivating the image of a folk philosopher, Frost skillfully avoided calling attention to the troubling complexity of his art. He wanted to be understood, but not easily, and he enjoyed playing the trickster to his audience. In a eulogy for Frost delivered in Amherst in October of 1963, President Kennedy called the poet "one of the granite figures of our time in America. . . . In honoring Robert Frost we therefore can pay honor to the deepest sources of our national strength." But Kennedy, speaking less than a month before his assassination, added, "If Robert Frost was much honored during his lifetime, it was because many preferred to ignore his darker truths."

Those darker truths include the uncertain relations between man and nature, the unending conflicts among men, the tensions that threaten marriage and home, and the limitations of human knowledge. Frost's poetry reveals fear, competition, and violence lurking beneath the eglitarian ideals of democracy, and a will to power hidden beneath jokes and light words. Approachability and clarity mask the complexity and strangeness of his poetry. "It takes all sorts of in and outdoor schooling/To get adapted to my kind of fooling," Frost wrote near the end of his life. A great deal of "in and outdoor schooling" informs his poetry from the beginning, and Frost's life is filled with the contradictions and tensions of both. As a poultry farmer, Frost wrote pastoral and georgic poetry, modes of contemplation and labor, in the tradition of Theocritus and Virgil, whom he read in the original. He memorized hundreds of the best English poems and wore copies of Shakespeare, Arnold, and Browning to tatters. As commanding a reader of Scripture as most theologians, he was also a passionate and learned botanist and amateur astronomer who maintained a lifelong dialogue with science and scientists. A provincial New Englander, he spent three years studying at Harvard and three years in England, where he immediately impressed the leading practitioners of modernism, Ezra Pound and William Butler Yeats. The man who was to become America's most widely read poet published his first book, *A Boy's Will,* in England at the age of nearly forty, his boyhood far behind him. His second book, *North of Boston,* which has been called "the most American of all modern books of poetry," was written mainly while he lived in England and also published there.

The great poet of New England Robert Lee Frost was born in San Francisco on March 26, 1874, and named after the leader of the Confederate Army, General Robert E. Lee. His father, William Prescott Frost, a Phi Beta Kappa graduate of Harvard, was an ambitious politico in the Democratic party and an aspiring journalist. Unsuccessful at both, he died of consumption when Robert was eleven, leaving the family broke. Isabelle Moodie, Frost's mother, was a deeply religious woman who baptized her son in the Swedenborgian church. After her husband's death she moved Robert and his sister, Jeannie, to New Hampshire, where she became a school-teacher. A first-rate student in high school, Robert was grad-uated at the top of his class, and was covaledictorian with his future wife, Elinor Miriam White. He also had begun writing poetry, publishing his first effort, "La Noche Triste," in the school newspaper. Despite his intellect and appetite for knowledge, Frost had little patience for college as he followed his developing talent for poetry and his passion for his fiancée. He enrolled at Dartmouth College and dropped out after less than a term, working then at odd jobs. After a tempestuous courtship, he finally married Elinor.

Indoor schooling remained important enough for Frost to try college again, though his motive appears to have been bolstering his credentials to teach secondary school. He en-tered Harvard College in 1898, where he studied historical geology with Nathaniel Southgate Shaler (something of the Stephen Jay Gould of his time), classics, and philosophy under George Santayana, Josiah Royce, George Herbert Palmer, and Hugo Münsterberg. Under Münsterberg, Frost read William James's *Psychology: A Briefer Course*, a work he would later teach to high school students. James's attempts to reconcile human consciousness and belief with science informed Frost's philosophical pragmatism, and the debates among those philosophers remained an important part of Frost's intellectual and imaginative development.

A superb student, Frost nevertheless left Harvard in 1900 somewhat impatient and under pressure from his own and his family's health problems (his doctor had warned him against being too sedentary). With the help of his maternal grandfather, Frost bought a poultry farm in 1900, the same year that he lost his mother to cancer and his four-year-old son, Elliott, to cholera. Despite depression and the demands of "hugger mugger" farming, Frost was writing poetry at night. He had a chapbook of a few early poems, entitled *Twilight*, privately published in 1894 and a few of his poems were published in magazines, most notably "My Butterfly: An Elegy" in Susan Hays Ward's *The Independent* (1894) and "The Tuft of Flowers" in the Derry *Enterprise* (1906). Though he continued to write while tending the farm, success in publication eluded Frost for nearly all of the first two decades as a poet.

Aided by his old high school friend Carl Burrell, Frost had also continued to develop his passion for botany. Throughout the nineteenth century botany was considered an important form of instruction in natural theology and God's designing providence, directed particularly at the moral education of young men and women. Frost loved the study of rare wild flowers, and orchids appear frequently in his poems. By the turn of the century botany had become increasingly influenced by science that revealed that the beauty of flowers had little to do with human sentiments or perfection but are temporary contrivances in a complex and changing game of procreation and survival. The maiming of an orchid lover is the subject of the "The Self-Seeker," a poem based on an incident in which Carl Burrell's legs were crushed in a box factory. But the dark saying of the poem, "pressed into service means pressed out of shape," reveals the way different forms of life, flowers and men, are part of a relentless machinery in which individual interests and desires are subsumed in a larger, if incomprehensible, process. Flowers in Frost become not only figures of beauty and of poetry but also of the elusive and troubling workings of both nature and God.

While managing several hundred hens, Frost also published a number of essays and stories in *Farm-Poultryman* magazine, some based on the efforts of his neighbor, John Hall, to breed prize hens. But Hall's appearance later in the poem "The Housekeeper" depicts a man obsessed with perfection and quite willing to let his farm go to hell. Frost was himself, by all accounts, an inept farmer; things went to ruin while he pursued his poetry. Frost exchanged his vocation as a "henman" with a career as a teacher at the Plymouth Normal School and the Pinkerton Academy in New Hampshire from 1906 until 1912. Both he and Elinor then made the romantic decision to sell their farm and "travel about the world a little." They moved their four children—daughters Leslie, Irma, Marjorie, and son, Carol—to England, where they remained until 1915.

In England, Frost befriended the essayist Edward Thomas, and their conversations led to the birth of Thomas's poetic career and the sure growth of Frost's own. Their long walks and conversations coincided with the development in Frost's poetry of a complex blend of dramatic narrative and dialogue. A mortar shell ended Thomas's life in World War I, and one of Frost's only elegies, "To E. T.," was written in his memory. Having met little success in getting individual poems published in the United States, Frost was able to assemble an entire collection and sought out an English publisher. In 1913, David Nutt brought out *A Boy's Will*, followed a year later by *North of Boston*. Both received numerous positive reviews, including one by the impresario and practitioner of literary high modernism, Ezra Pound. Frost met and sparred with major players in the British literary scene, including Pound, William Butler Yeats, Ford Maddox Ford, and T. E. Hulme, all of whom, with a certain measure of condescension, found his poetry superb. Pound, an expatriate native of Idaho, was giddy over having "just discovered another Amur'kn. VURRY Amu'k'n, with, I think, the seeds of grace." Pound advised Harriet Monroe, editor of the prestigious journal *Poetry*, to print his review of Frost's first book "at once as we ought to be first and some of the reviewers here are sure to make fuss enough to get quoted in N.Y." Patronizing and opportunistic though he may have been, Pound knew, as he had when he first encountered the work of T. S. Eliot, a good thing when he saw it. By the time of his return to the United States in 1915, Frost had become a poet of considerable note, and Henry Holt was eager to publish his books. After the publication of *Mountain Interval* in 1916, he was offered a one-semester teaching position at Amherst, which he eventually quit in 1920 after disagreements with the president, Alexander Meiklejohn. From then on Frost would spend his time in and out of visiting professorships at prestigious universities. His reputation grew to national and global proportions, fueled both by the power of his work and also by his success as a performer and raconteur. The twenty years of relative isolation and anonymity that had produced some of the most engaging and innovative poetry of the twentieth century were over.

Frost was an unassuming innovator, though a great one. More than any poet except Shakespeare, he brought the possibilities of English meters and the rhythms of ordinary speech together with exquisite skill, power, and subtlety. Rarely calling attention to his own technical brilliance Frost chose to lure the reader into his labyrinth, allowing his poetry's strangeness and complexity to work gradually upon the

imagination. If the self-exiled Americans Ezra Pound and
T. S. Eliot were showing their contempt for America and
democracy by crafting a poetry incomprehensible to the com-
mon reader, Frost desired to contain his vision in art that did
not call attention to its artfulness. He appealed to a democratic
audience in part because of a strong belief that all humanity
shared thoughts and desires in common, even if only a few
had the skill or the courage to reveal them in literature. He
once said of his own work, "I should like to be so subtle at
this game as to seem to the casual observer altogether obvi-
ous." One of his great predecessors, Emily Dickinson, wrote,
"Tell all the truth but tell it slant." Frost found his own way
of telling the truth slant, obliquely, embracing all of its com-
plexity. Frost emphasized the importance of metaphor in all
ranges of thought, and he loved the way metaphor could both
"say one thing in terms of another" but also "say one thing
and mean another." Metaphor and poetry become ways of
both concealing and revealing, the way the wall does in his
famous poem "Mending Wall." Frost expressed this tension
in a letter to a friend: "I have written to keep the curious out
of the secret places of my mind both in my verse and in my
letters to such as you." Yet Frost's writing, approachable and
beguiling, presents an invitation to the secret places of his
mind. Frost did develop a relationship, though a diabolical
one, with his audience: "My poems . . . are all set to trip the
reader head foremost into the boundless. Ever since infancy I
have had the habit of leaving my blocks carts chairs and such
like ordinaries where people would be pretty sure to fall for-
ward over them and in the dark. Forward, you understand,
and in the dark."

Unlike the urban visions of Eliot, Crane, and Stevens,
Frost's poetry strikes the reader first and foremost as being
about country life and about nature, and he focused on aspects
of both "common in life but uncommon in poetry." His

work appears to evoke the pastoral ideals of rural independence that had been advocated by Thomas Jefferson. And it invites us to read nature as a purifying scripture and symbol of the spirit, as it had been by the American sages Ralph Waldo Emerson and Henry David Thoreau, both of whom Frost read and admired. But, once taken in, we find Frost's country world pervaded by struggle, limitation, ambiguity, and evil. And Frost's vision is always complicated by the drama of the observer in interpreting any fact or situation.

Frost appears to urge, as he titled one poem, "The Need of Being Versed in Country Things." The title tells us a great deal about the trickiness and subtlety of Frost's work. Sounding like an invitation to homespun country wisdom, the title wryly alludes to Prince Hamlet's response to Ophelia: "Do you think I meant country matters?" In the Elizabethan world, "country matters" implied "something indecent." To an audience accustomed to poetry that pointed to nature as a source of solace or transcendent revelation, Frost no doubt meant something indecent by a poem that describes the inexplicable destruction of a farm by fire, its use by birds who "rejoice in the nest they kept" indifferent to human loss, and its rebuke of human sentimentality "dwelling too much on what has been." "Versed," a colloquialism that means "taught" or "schooled," casually raises a question that haunts Frost's work: What is the relation of poetry, "verse," to knowledge of the world? If poetry had become the repository for sentiments and emotion, Frost's poem suggests the need to unlearn our emotions in order to accept and survive in life's cruelty. Our having "to be versed in country things/*Not* to believe the phoebes wept," [emphasis mine] reflects the difficulty of accommodating human beliefs and desires to the indifference and coldness of the world.

Frost's thoughtful and subversive attitude about country matters can be seen very clearly in a little-known interview.

Asked whether he thought nature was cruel or not, Frost's anecdotal answer reveals much about his ironic stance toward an educated and genteel audience. He takes exception with the view held by Matthew Arnold that nature is cruel and that man is somehow morally superior. But he takes special care to poke fun at an American minister and professor expounding to students on the peacefulness and beauty of nature:

> I know it [nature] isn't kind. As Matthew Arnold said: "Nature is cruel. It's man that's sick of blood." And it doesn't seem very sick of it. Nature is always more or less cruel. Shall I tell you what happened on the porch of a professor—minister he was, too? The war was going on, a beautiful moonlit night. He was there with some boys, talking about the horrors of war—how cruel men were to each other and how kind nature was, what a beautiful country this was spread beneath us, you know—moonlight on it. And just as he talked that way, spreading his arm over it, a bird began to shriek down in the woods—something had got into its nest. Nature was being cruel. The woods are killing each other anyway. That's where the expression came from "a place in the sun." A tree wanting a place in the sun it can't get. The other trees won't give it to it.

Nature includes human nature, and both are always "more or less cruel." The difference between the human and non-human world often blurs in Frost's work in ways that are both comforting and disturbing. In Frost, human consciousness does not alone embrace emotions and moral sensibility, and he explores the relation of our consciousness to that of other species brilliantly in "The Need of Being Versed in Country Things" and also in "Range-Finding" and "The Oven Bird."

One can see the complexity of his treatment of the relations of man and nonhuman nature in the memorable little poem

"Dust of Snow," originally titled "A Favour." The sudden disturbance of snow by a crow somehow changes the speaker's mood, "saving" something from a troubled past. As is the case in almost all Frost's poetry, the details and the tone demand further attention:

> The way a crow
> Shook down on me
> The dust of snow
> From a hemlock tree
>
> Has given my heart
> A change of mood
> And saved some part
> Of a day I had rued.

The poem represents a great technical achievement, turning the subject and predicate of a single sentence of mostly monosyllables into a supple rhythmic revelation. It has roundness, closure, and denouement. But Frost had little patience for the kind of pleasure of pure form as an end in itself—what he called "that Beauty is Truth claptrap." Frost wrote to a friend, "My object is true form—is was and always will be—form true to any chance bit of true life." In "Dust of Snow," "true life" remains elusive, if still demanding both the speaker's and the reader's interpretation. Here the movement of a black crow disturbs the still blankness of snow. In two other important poems, "The Tuft of Flowers" and "The Wood-Pile," the sudden flight of a butterfly and a small bird, respectively, signify to observers the portent of a message. In those poems, as in "Dust of Snow," there is a question of how personally one should take such an event. A crow may have "shook down" the "dust of snow" on the speaker, but was the "way" it happened the result of the crow being scared by the speaker's presence or part of a process of loosening hemlock seeds to be eaten? The shift in tenses suggests that the change of mood was not immediate. What does venturing into nature teach us? Crow, hemlock (associated with poison), and the analogy of snow and "dust" seem particularly ominous. How could this event save "some part" of a day he had "rued"? Does it recall something bad or preserve a good part of an otherwise intolerable memory?

Frost always enjoyed working within traditions, creating meaning through subtle dialogue with his predecessors. Once asked how he became a poet, Frost replied, "I followed the procession down the ages." Thomas Hardy's poem "In a Wood," for example, provides a similar drama, in which the speaker learns something from nature that makes life more tolerable. And it comes as a surprise that neither nature's beauty nor its serenity, but its quiet violence, provides some revelation. Hardy knew what Frost knew about the way trees fight:

> But, having entered in,
>   Great growths and small
> Show them to men akin—
>   Combatants all!
> Sycamore shoulders oak,
>   Bines the slim sapling yoke,
> Ivy-spun halters choke
>   Elms stout and tall.

The wanderer's perception of nature's cruelty leads to the revelation that at least the human world might provide more, or at least some solace after all. Something could be saved by returning to humanity if one recognizes the terror in the rest of nature:

> *Since, then, no grace I find*
> *Taught me of trees,*
> *Turn I back to my kind,*
> *Worthy as these.*
> *There at least smiles abound,*
> *There discourse trills around,*
> *There, now and then, are found*
> *Life-loyalties.*

Frost's conclusion in "Dust of Snow" may be more ambiguous than Hardy's, perhaps accepting of what are only "now and then" "Life-loyalties." Hemlock trees kill anything that grow in their shade. Crows eat the seeds that burst from the hemlock's buds in winter. Birth, death, competition, and struggle found in nature mute the excesses of regret over the pain we find in human life.

The title of Frost's first book, *A Boy's Will*, and its keynote poem, "Into My Own," evoke an American faith in the heroic qualities of the youthful individual, escaping the bonds and mediocrity of traditional society and heading out into the territory ahead; he follows the liberating mission of the Puritans and their "errand into the wilderness." From the beginning, Frost's handling of this American mythology is fraught with ironies that suggest not "rugged" but what he called "ragged individualism." In "Into My Own," the speaker cannot *do* anything, only "wish" it. "Will" manifests its destiny only in the form of the hypothetical "should" and "would":

> *I should not be withheld but that some day*
> *Into their vastness I should steal away,*
> *Fearless of ever finding open land,*
> *Or highway where the slow wheel pours the sand.*

I do not see why I should e'er turn back,
Or those should not set forth upon my track
To overtake me, who should miss me here
And long to know if still I held them dear.

Though he doesn't see why he "should e'er turn back," the thoughts of those "who should miss me here/And long to know if still I held them dear" remind him and the reader of the persistence of what he wishes to escape, of the real hold that others have upon the self. The desire for individual freedom in Frost always meets the challenges of our need to be social, to be loved, and sets limits on going too far in thought and in art. As he wrote in appreciation of the poetry of Amy Lowell: "The most exciting movement in nature is not progress, advance, but expansion and contraction, the opening and shutting of the eye, the hand, the heart, the mind. We throw our arms wide with a gesture of religion to the universe; we close them around a person. We explore and adventure for a while and then we draw in to consolidate our gains. The breathless swing is between subject matter and form." And the adventure would produce nothing but the testing of convictions which he had from the beginning—or so he hopes: "They would not find me changed from him they knew—/Only more sure of all I thought was true." This vision of a heroic individual wandering in the wilderness is tested in a number of poems in *A Boy's Will* and in his subsequent books: "A Dream Pang," "The Demiurge's Laugh," "The Trial by Existence," "Reluctance," and later "The Wood-Pile," "Stopping by Woods on a Snowy Evening," and, of course, "The Road Not Taken."

If the myth of the independent pilgrim was part of the myth of America, it was also part of a Christian idea of spiritual progress and redemption. Frost, however, saw this Christian pilgrimage in terms of torture, suffering, and uncertainty, a trial testing faith to its limits. Such is the way "The Trial by Existence" concludes, a poem in which life takes on meaning only through "earthly woe" and "agony of strife" without even the heroic pride of wisdom and choice:

> But always God speaks at the end:
>> "One thought in agony of strife
> The bravest would have by for friend,
>> The memory that he chose the life;
> But the pure fate to which you go
>> Admits no memory of choice,
> Or the woe were not earthly woe
>> To which you give the assenting voice."

Meaningful spiritual experience for Frost recognizes the limits of reason and the need to find "The mystic link to bind and hold/Spirit to matter till death come." What comes after death cannot be known, otherwise spiritual struggle would be hollow. The poem concludes with a terrifying recognition of the way life's trials destroy pride but still underscores our mysterious responsibility for what "we somehow chose":

> 'Tis of the essence of life here,
>> Though we choose greatly, still to lack
> The lasting memory at all clear,
>> That life has for us on the wrack
> Nothing but what we somehow chose;
>> Thus are we wholly stripped of pride
> In the pain that has but one close,
>> Bearing it crushed and mystified.

The meaning of that "one close" hardly guarantees redemption; in earth or in heaven, we "find that the utmost reward/Of daring should be still to dare." The self-assured march of "The Trial by Existence" into uncertainty and the bewilderment of being "mystified" foreshadows the tensions and ironies of Frost's most famous pilgrimage poem, "The Road Not Taken." The drama of choosing direction at a crossroads is a commonplace, but Frost's poem evokes the agonies of similar scenes in the Bible, Sophocles, Dante, Dickinson (poem 615, with "that odd Fork in Being's Road"), as well as Thoreau's faith in the magnetism of nature in his essay "Walking." How much choice is there when we learn that both roads had been worn about the same, not to mention that they already exist as paths and that they are covered with leaves? The speaker will not know until "ages and ages hence" what "difference," if any, has been made—only retrospect gives the sense of destiny or of design. And the speaker will be telling it with "a sigh," perhaps as much from pain as from relief, as much for regret about the road not taken as for the road he took.

Often enough in Frost human will is set against the challenges of a larger chaos. The conflict of will and environment—or will against will—is suggested in the muted allusion of the title *A Boy's Will* to Longfellow's "My Lost Youth." Frost echoes the line "A boy's will is the wind's will,/And the thoughts of youth are long, long thoughts," and in so doing reveals his desire to work within a popular "fireside" tradition while also subverting it. How much force does the individual will have against the chaotic forces of the "wind's will"? Frost once wrote that all his poems "are figures of the great predicament, the will braving alien entanglements." In "The Need of Being Versed in Country Things," we learn that in addition to a house that burned down, the "barn opposed across the way" would have "joined the house in flame/Had it been the will of the wind." Capricious and destructive, the wind becomes a figure of chance and change that also suggests the incomprehensible and manifestly inhuman presence Job heard and saw from the whirlwind. Wind figures powerfully in many of the poems of *A Boy's Will*, including "Storm Fear," "To the Thawing Wind," "A Line-Storm Song," "Reluctance," and "Pan with Us," in which Pan, the ancient god of nature and of poetry, recognizes sadly that the poet's pipes have little more power to stir than "the merest aimless breath of air." Yet, in "To the Thawing Wind," the speaker enlists the wind's power to threaten his comfort and drive him into nature: "Melt the glass and leave the sticks/Like a hermit's crucifix;/Burst into my narrow stall;/Swing the picture on the wall;/Run the rattling pages o'er;/Scatter poems on the floor;/Turn the poet out of door." The stunning poems with which the volume concludes— "Now Close the Windows," "A Line-Storm Song," "October," "My Butterfly," and "Reluctance"—all take the will of the wind as a blind demiurge of life, death, and loss in the figures of scattered flowers and dead leaves. In "A Line-Storm Song," the wind and storm suggest the threat and fear of primordial extinction against which love must work:

> Oh, never this whelming east wind swells
>   But it seems like the sea's return
> To the ancient lands where it left the shells
>   Before the age of the fern;
> And it seems like the time when after doubt
>   Our love came back amain.
> Oh, come forth into the storm and rout
>   And be my love in the rain.

The power of love here is invoked against the extinguishing threat of deluge; love returns to overcome the ancient threat. *A Boy's Will* concludes with "Reluctance," the heart and the will resisting "the end/Of a love or a season," as the speaker is worn down at the end of his journey. The speaker, like the leaves, has suffered a fall, and the breaking of will. Reluctant to give up, he meditates on the tension between the heart's desire and the limits of the physical body, captured in the grim pun of choice, "whither":

> And the dead leaves lie huddled and still,
>   No longer blown hither and thither;
> The last lone aster is gone;
>   The flowers of the witch-hazel wither;
> The heart is still aching to seek,
>   But the feet question "Whither?"

A Boy's Will begins and ends with poems about journeys. But the journey remains circular, following not a linear path but a cycling of seasons that begins and ends with autumn, that mythically provocative season of the fall.

In Genesis God breathed on the dust and made man a living soul. Frost often meditates on an old controversy of whether that "soul" and God's "breath" are merely wind destined to die with the body. In Latin, the word for spirit, *spiritus*, is also the word for breath, wind, and inspiration. "The Aim Was Song" wavers between an affirmation and a parody of the romantic notion that man and art are the evolutionary fulfillment of nature's inspiration. Perhaps we are only presences creating momentary order from otherwise indifferent forces. With dramatic extravagance that veers toward a fallacious just-so story, we learn that the "wind once blew itself untaught," and then "Man came to tell it what was wrong":

> He took a little in his mouth,
>   And held it long enough for north
> To be converted into south,
>   And then by measure blew it forth.

> *By measure. It was word and note,*
>   *The wind the wind had meant to be—*
> *A little through the lips and throat.*
>   *The aim was song—the wind could see.*

The line "The wind the wind had meant to be"—with its repetition and monosyllables—seems to force intention and meaning to the brink of tautology (as does the remarkable fifteenth line of the sonnet "Hyla Brook": "We love the things we love for what they are."). The phrase "a little through the lips and throat" sounds like a mock advertisement for gum or chewing tobacco. Be that as may be, "the lips and throat" are not the soul or the will but the body acting as small, physical instrument. If the "aim was song," was it really the wind's or just our own? The final phrase of the poem "the wind could see" (for it sees nothing) is an example of the way Frost pricks the balloon of our desire to see our aims confirmed by nature or by God.

Frost's poetry does reflect an interest in other creatures and in their primordial sounds as a source of meaning. The sonnet "The Oven Bird" represents the voice of a stoic creature, surviving and creating meaningful sound in a difficult environment. Frost insisted on creating fresh meaning while working within such traditional and demanding forms as the sonnet or the iambic pentameter line; it reinforced the sense of both tension and limitation that he found challenging and exciting in life. Both indoor and outdoor schooling help in understanding the poem. The song of oven birds rises suddenly and sharply before falling, ending in a repetitive utterance that sounds, suggestively, like "preacher, preacher, preacher." Darwin describes how oven birds build their nests, which look like human homes, on the ground with both inner and outer chambers. In addition to the North American warbler, Frost also wryly alludes to Darwin's discussion of the oven bird, from the genus *Furnarius*, in *The Voyage of the Beagle*. Darwin considered it one of those creatures that might eventually reveal the way all species are related. In the same book Darwin discusses the songs of little Hyla frogs, the subject of the sonnet "Hyla Brook" that Frost paired with "The Oven Bird" in *Mountain Interval*. Frost loved *The Voyage of the Beagle* (he owned three copies), and the pairing of the two poems reveals the subtle way Frost draws complex material into his poetry without encumbering its aural effect. The sonnet's octave suggests the rejuvenating power of the oven bird's song:

> There is a singer everyone has heard,
> Loud, a mid-summer and a mid-wood bird,
> Who makes the solid tree trunks sound again.
> He says that leaves are old and that for flowers
> Mid-summer is to spring as one to ten.

But as the bird's song drops, the sonnet turns on the line that begins the concluding sestet: "And comes that other fall we name the fall," and we learn of the oven bird's ability to sing when other birds have gone silent by not quite singing:

> And comes that other fall we name the fall.
> He says the highway dust is over all.
> The bird would cease and be as other birds
> But that he knows in singing not to sing.
> The question that he frames in all but words
> Is what to make of a diminished thing.

The repetition of "the fall" evokes not only the oncoming season but, wryly, the biblical Fall. But "the fall" is part of the mythology created by our names. The oven bird's question in "all but words" indicates the superfluousness of words before the power of primordial, creaturely sound. One of the issues raised by the poem is whether our Judeo-Christian stories of loss and redemption can continue to have meaning in a world of common creaturely descent and constant struggle, the world of Darwin. The poem also describes the tension between linear time and cyclical time. And the question so framed is how to interpret such a world, this "diminished thing." Frost uses the word "thing" and its variant "something" throughout his poetry in a brilliant way that reflects the elusiveness of reality and the inadequacy of our names. Little things in Frost stand as parts or samples reflecting a larger whole: "I believe in what the Greeks called synecdoche: the philosophy of the part for the whole; skirting the hem of the goddess. All that an artist needs is samples." Later, he wrote setting him apart from his modernist contemporaries, "I started calling myself a synecdochist when others called themselves Imagists or Vorticists. . . . Always a larger significance. A little thing touches a larger thing." Frost no doubt worked in a rhetorical tradition of romantic thought that William Blake announced in the first aphorism of "Auguries of Innocence": "To see a World in a Grain of Sand/And a Heaven in a Wild Flower/Hold Infinity in the palm of your hand/And Eternity in an Hour." But Frost also doubted that a "World," "Infinity," or "Eternity" could be found in the facts of the world. Nature's flux may not reveal "Truth," but at least, as he wrote, "For once, then, something."

The importance of sound in Frost extends deep into the realm of human relations. During his years in England, he revealed in letters the emphasis he had begun to place on the dramatic tones of talk and the posturing of the human voice in the creation of meaning. In 1914, he wrote to his former student John Bartlett; "I give you a new definition of a sentence: A sentence is a sound on which other sounds called words may be strung." He wanted to capture "the sounds of sense with all their irregularity of accent across the regular beat of the meter." Frost's insights coincided with an emphasis on drama and speech, recognizing that meaning is created through dialogue and conversation. Meaning is dramatic, and words and sentences are ultimately deeds. Frost liked to "say" poems, not "read" them, because of his emphasis on the dramatic life and flexibility of meaning through sentence sounds and voice posturing. Meaning was not inherent in words alone or beyond them but in the tension between words and the undercurrent of dramatic tones on which the words flowed. Frost saw colloquy and dialogue as a metaphor for the struggle and agon of creation, the creation and destruction of masks and postures in the play of existence. Poems in which characters appear have obscure and different ways of looking at the world—"Mending Wall," "The Code," "The Mountain," "Home Burial"—reveal much more about themselves and their motives through their tone. In the early poem "Revelation," Frost asserts the limits of masquerade and mystery "Behind light words that tease and flout," recognizing in the end that ". . . all, from babes that play/At hide-and-seek to God afar,/So all who hide too well away/Must speak and tell us where they are." And when they speak, it is the tone that speaks and not only the rhetorical postures of words.

Frost's dramatic poetry finds full development in *North of Boston*—narratives, dramatic monologues, ballads—all of which really draw on the ancient form of poetic dialogue known as eclogue, a debate between shepherds or rustics that explores the relations of work and play, haves and have-nots, power and fear. The only traditional lyric in *North of Boston* is "After Apple-Picking"; aside from the stunning dramatic monologue "A Servant to Servants," all of the other poems are strikingly original hybrids of narrative, lyric, and dialogue that heighten the importance of circumstance and perspective in an ongoing drama of life. The tensions between characters in these poems reveal the instability of hierarchies and the tentativeness of power and control. In "The Tuft of Flowers" of *A Boy's Will*, a farmworker whose task is to turn the hay after the mower has cut it asserts the bond between himself and his fellow worker: " 'Men work together,' I told him from the heart,/'Whether they work together or apart.' " A footnote to "Mending Wall" in the first edition of *North of Boston* stated, " 'Mending Wall' takes up the theme where the 'Tuft of Flowers' in *A Boy's Will* laid it down." Throughout the book, Frost addresses the possibility of shared experience of both work and play among men and women despite an uneasy awareness of life's challenges and an anxiety about power and lack of equality. Frost enjoyed saying, "I am a great equalitarian. I try to spend most of my time with my equals." Hardly an egalitarian, Frost nevertheless saw the way in which all human beings participate in what he called the "ritualism of nature," its outdoor games for mortal stakes. In several of his narrative and eclogue poems, Frost's most compelling characters are French-Canadian. Frost acknowledged that the character of "the old-stone savage" of "Mending Wall" and Baptiste of "The Ax-Helve" were inspired by a French-Canadian farmer named Napoleon Guay. Lafayette of "A Hundred Collars" enjoys teasing and threatening Professor Magoon (his name is telling) while finding his own wily ways to making a living and garnering power. The fact of the severe racism experienced by French-Canadians (related to a Protestant demonization of Catholics) haunts these poems. The "civilized" Yankee characters in these poems reveal their fears of losing power to their more "savage," though often shrewder and wise, French-Canadian interlocutors. Unwilling to be sentimental about human nature, Frost depicts cunning and self-deception in all ranges of human life.

The speaker of "Mending Wall," for example, appears

something of a liberal in his disdain of walls, beginning the poem by saying, "Something there is that doesn't love a wall." But the speaker is not Frost. Rather, the poem reveals a conflict of "sayings": "Something there is that doesn't love a wall" is balanced by the competing line of the neighbor, " 'Good fences make good neighbors.' " The irony of the poem becomes apparent when we realize that it is the speaker who initiates the mending, the "re-pairing." And his own openness appears contradicted by his disdain for hunters who knock the wall down: "The work of hunters is another thing:/I have come after them and made repair/Where they have left not one stone on a stone,/But they would have the rabbit out of hiding,/To please the yelping dogs." Is the work of hunters "another," a different sort of, thing from what the "frozen-ground-swell" does subtly to the wall, or just one more thing or force? This vigorous aside unmasks the speaker's none-too-populist and egalitarian attitude. His contempt and fear of his neighbor and his desire to maintain his own place in an imagined hierarchy of being lead him to call the French-Canadian "an old-stone savage armed," a primitive clinging to his relics. But the truth of what this "savage" says is borne out in the drama of the poem. Good fences do make good neighbors because they allow for colloquy while also keeping privacy and individuality. Despite their seemingly different positions, both men are leveled equal by the fact that they play the same "outdoor game,/One on a side," though it is, as Frost would write later, "play for mortal stakes."

The survival of home and the future is at stake in Frost's representation of the conflict between men and women. If love poetry had traditionally involved the address of a single speaker to his absent lover, Frost's development of a poetry in which women have an equal and great presence may be one of his most important contributions to modern poetry. His portraits of women in "A Servant to Servants" (a dramatic

monologue), "The Witch of Coös," "Home Burial," "The
Fear," "In the Home Stretch," or "Wild Grapes" are among
the greatest and most complex in English poetry. Often Frost
appears to speak through these women, and they are not, as
some have argued, merely mad or tricksters but powerful eth-
ical figures who subvert the control and reveal the cruelty of
those around them. In "Wild Grapes," the woman narrator
resists the reductive instructions of her brother to hang on to
her passions and dreams. She has no desire to let go with the
heart, even to the point of uselessness and death. The speaker
of a "Servant to Servants" reasons because she suffers, and her
story becomes a moving example for the botanizers on her
doorstep of a soul attempting to maintain itself despite the
curse of heredity and the cruelty of her husband. "The Gen-
erations of Men" finds a powerful girl teasing a boy with
Hamlet-like cleverness and dissembling—in the game of
courtship, she exercises the power of choice. The power of
women to choose and control the world as well as the sadness
at the loss of that power lurks beneath the masquerades of
"The Witch of Coös" and "The Pauper Witch of Grafton."
In its explorations of the mythologies of women and nature,
the deceptions and insights of naming, and the limits of human
control, "Maple" remains an unacknowledged masterpiece.

Frost's conception of life as a conversation that refuses clo-
sure informs his dramatic dialogues between men and women.
Some of the most convincing and disturbing colloquies in
Frost occur between men and women, particularly in "Home
Burial, "In the Home Stretch," "The Fear," and "The Death
of the Hired Man." What it means to be human becomes
worked out in the conflict of these conversations. In "The
Death of the Hired Man," the nature and stability of "home,"
itself a metaphor for order, finds meaning only tentatively in
the debate between Mary and her husband, Warren. Frost
breaks the blank verse line (unrhymed iambic pentameter)

across the initial statements of both, allowing each voice to play in variations before falling back into the regular meter that acts as the life pulse. Frost said there are only two meters in English, "strict iambic" and "loose iambic," and here he demonstrates the way thought plays within the rhythms of ordinary speech but still follows a very regular and powerful cadence that sometimes resists but ultimately falls into the regularity of iambic pentameter:

> *"Home," he mocked gently.*
>
> > > > *"Yes, what else but home?*
> *It all depends on what you mean by home.*
> *Of course he's nothing to us, any more*
> *Than was the hound that came a stranger to us*
> *Out of the woods, worn out upon the trail."*
>
> *"Home is the place where, when you have to go there,*
> *They have to take you in."*
>
> > > > *"I should have called it*
> *Something you somehow haven't to deserve."*

This dialogue arrives at different and troubling attitudes toward home as Mary and Warren work out their thoughts in reaction to each other's cues. But the momentary points of agreement can be destroyed if the wills of the players fail to accommodate each other. That failure is implied in the dark pun of the title of "Home Burial," one of Frost's greatest poems. The death of a child makes participation in the ordinary rhythms of life nearly impossible and reveals hidden faults in the souls of a husband and wife. Amy and her husband know how to hurt each other, and the questioning of the reality of each other's grief becomes a pretext for fear-driven displays of power and control. Amy accuses her husband of not knowing how to grieve, while also refusing his attempts to understand her grief. In "Home Burial" great demands are placed on both the characters and the reader to interpret the tone in order to understand what is being said. Is the husband really a brute, treading crudely on his wife's profound grief over the loss of a child? Or does Amy's silence and anger reflect grief about her marriage and her husband's control over her? Each finds ways of destroying the barriers the other creates in an ongoing drama of power. Much depends upon how we take the husband's tone when he says:

> The little graveyard where my people are!
> So small the window frames the whole of it.
> Not so much larger than a bedroom, is it?

The analogy between the bedroom and the graveyard has inspired much interpretation. Is he clumsy or deliberately and cruelly reminding her of her place in relation to *his* purposes? Is there a suggestion here about sexual frigidity or a reminder of how this represents *his* family portrait? Amy had heard her husband say while he was digging the child's grave, " 'Three foggy mornings and one rainy day/Will rot the best birch fence a man can build.' " She assumes he merely speaks of "everyday concerns." But the tone with which he said it could transform it into a muted and powerful, if not terrifying, metaphor for both his dead child and his marriage—a barrier against the future and against the moral authority of his wife. Amy's grief is not a mystery but a weapon, a possession, and a barrier she builds while reducing her husband to being crude and subhuman. In retaliation he seems to grant her superiority while simultaneously pointing to her inhumanity: " 'Tell me about it if it's something human./Let me into your grief.' " Frost's quest is to understand in the chaotic and threatening worlds in and outside the home what it means to be human.

Frost enjoyed dialogue and conflict not only from his hatred of the tyranny of utopia but also from a deeper fear of solitude. Two of Frost's best lyrics, "Mowing" and "After Apple-Picking," force us to see not only the individual laborer but also the limits and futility of man alone in the universe (one of the laborers uses a "long scythe" and the other a "long two-pointed ladder" as an instrument of perception), straining at the limits with no response from man or God. In "Mowing," cutting the hay and leaving it "to make"—that is, to dry in the sun—are some of the fundamental forms of farm labor. The poem has been taken as a work about poetry—about the satisfactions of combining work and play through the creation of a comforting sound and rhythm, and this is partly true. But as in almost all of Frost, the expectation and even first appearance of comfort cannot hide what so troubles the laborer's daydreaming. The loneliness of the speaker is more than apparent in his opening line: "There never was a sound beside the wood but one,/And that was my long scythe whispering to the ground." The image of the cultivated field next to the wood suggests an unhappy Arcadia or garden, one devoid of anything but the man-made sound, incomprehensible even to the laborer himself. If the sonnet often attempts to resolve into comfort or affirmation of love, both are hard-won here. As a figure of the seeker looking for revelation in nature, the poem seems to provide only an ironic echo of the voice crying in the wilderness in Isaiah 40: "All flesh is grass, and all the goodliness thereof is as the flower of the field . . . the grass withereth, the flower fadeth: but the word of God shall stand forever." But here the only voice remains the whispering of the laborer's scythe, an instrument of order and destruction. This garden demands labor, already has technology, and encompasses creation as well as time and death for which the mower himself has often been a metaphor. "Something" keeps the scythe from "speaking," and we learn that it may be "something about the heat of the sun," suggestive of the power of the environment and the fact that man must labor by the sweat of his brow. Outdoor schooling tells more. The mower's "earnest love" lays the swale in rows and cuts down "feeble-pointed spikes of flowers/(Pale orchises), and scared a bright green snake." To a farmer, the flourishing of flowers represents an ironic curse of cultivation; flowers grow stronger as the cultivation continues. (In "A Star in a Stone-Boat," the farmer feels cursed that "The very nature of the soil was hot/ /And burning to yield flowers instead of grain,/Flowers fanned and not put out by all the rain/Poured on them by his prayers prayed in vain.") The flowers represent beauty and frustration. And their "feeble" presence as well as the failure of a "bright green snake" to remain camouflaged suggests the tentative presence of all life forms in a world of randomness and waste. All these "facts" prevent the mower's "dream" from growing too great, and the speaker arrives at the complex epiphany of acceptance: "The fact is the sweetest dream that labor knows." The facts hold only the hint of possible transcendence and are inextricably related to the senses and sensuous experience. The following line continues the action of labor that does not look too far into the future but only to the next step in the process of harvesting: "My long scythe whispered and left the hay to make," which may be all that can be said or done for the moment. With its unusual rhyme scheme, skeptical tones, and haunting sighing sounds, the poem allows for pain but does not drift into resentment— rather into a hard-won acceptance.

"After Apple-Picking" deepens the questions and fears raised in "Mowing," as it, too, weds fact and dream in a precarious drama of uncertainty. The exhaustion and acceptance of limits in the pursuit of perfection spur the speaker's meditation on desire and waste. Here, as in "Mowing," an irregular rhyme scheme draws the reader forward but under-scores the sense of uncertainty and swaying, as do the brilliantly varied line lengths such as "But I was well/Upon my way to sleep before it fell,/And I could tell/What form my dreaming was about to take." The repetition of sleep four times in the final five lines, as well as the pointed rhyme of the final word "sleep" with "heap," adds to the ominousness with which the poem concludes. The image of apple-picking invokes the fall of man through desire and knowledge, and the ladder recalls the biblical story of Jacob's dream of ascending and descending angels, as well as his wrestling with the angel of God. The word "heaven" in the second line is perhaps the only overt indication in the poem that this day's labor has something to do with the desire to find God or attain grace through labor in the world, a desire doomed to failure because of the inescapable limits of creaturely natures. The ladder had also become a figure for the scale of nature and the possibility of human progress. Swaying as it does in "After Apple-Picking" against the tree, it gives us a sense of man's precarious position in a vast, nearly inexhaustible world that grows and wastes, in which some are selected and others go to "the cider-apple heap/As of no worth." What may "trouble" the speaker's "human" sleep is that it serves no purpose other than to keep him on the ladder in pursuit of perfection, unlike the woodchuck, whose long sleep has at least preserved him in the safety of hibernation.

The fact of waste in creation is something Frost wanted to accept as both the joy and sadness of existence on earth. The motions of such a world do not imply progress but variations within cycles of growth and decay and competition—even among seemingly innocent forms—for a place in the sun.

In "After Apple-Picking" and in "Birches" (as well as "Wild Grapes"), the trees of life and of knowledge combine in a garden that never was and never will be perfect. Moments of skillful play are the best way to create, as he called it, "a momentary stay against confusion." In "Birches," the speaker, "weary of considerations," dreams of such a momentary stay through the boyhood memory of swinging on birch trees. The boy climbs only "Toward heaven," letting go and returning to earth because "Earth's the right place for love." And even though he knows how imperfect love can be—from the excesses of cruelty, selfishness, and desire—he admits, "I don't know where it's likely to go better." Frost expresses both the power and limitations of art in the concluding line "One could do worse than be a swinger of birches." As a poet, one has rarely done better.

SUGGESTIONS FOR
FURTHER READING

Bagby, George. *Robert Frost and the Book of Nature.* Knoxville: University of Tennessee Press, 1993.

Barron, Jonathan, and Earl Wilcox, eds. *Roads Not Taken: Rereading on Robert Frost.* Columbia: University of Missouri Press, 2000.

Brodsky, Joseph, Seamus Heaney, and Derek Walcott. *Homage to Robert Frost.* New York: Farrar, Straus and Giroux, 1996.

Brower, Reuben. *The Poetry of Robert Frost: Constellations of Intention.* Oxford: Oxford University Press, 1963.

Buxton, Rachel. *Robert Frost and Northern Irish Poetry.* Oxford: Oxford University Press, 2004.

Cady, Edwin H., and Louis J. Budd, eds. *On Frost.* Durham: Duke University Press, 1991.

Cook, Reginald. *Robert Frost: A Living Voice.* Amherst: University of Massachusetts Press, 1980.

Faggen, Robert. *Robert Frost and the Challenge of Darwin.* Ann Arbor: University of Michigan Press, 1997.

Faggen, Robert, ed. *The Cambridge Companion to Robert Frost.* Cambridge: Cambridge University Press, 2001.

Gerber, Philip. *Robert Frost.* New York: Twayne, 1966.

Hall, Dorothy Judd. *Contours of Belief.* Athens, Ohio: Ohio University Press, 1984.

Hass, Robert Bernard. *Going by Contraries: Frost's Conflict with Science.* Charlottesville: The University of Virginia Press, 2002.

Hoffman, Tyler. *Robert Frost and the Politics of Poetry.* Hanover: The University of New England Press, 2001.

Ingebretsen, Ed. *Robert Frost's Star in a Stone-boat: A Grammar of Belief.* San Francisco: Catholic Scholars Press, 1994.

Jost, Walter. *Rhetorical Investigations.* Charlottesville: The University of Virginia Press, 2004.

Kearns, Katherine. *Robert Frost and a Poetics of Appetite.* Cambridge: Cambridge University Press, 1994.

Kilcup, Karen. *Robert Frost and Feminine Literary Tradition.* Ann Arbor: The University of Michigan Press, 1999.

Lentricchia, Frank. *Modernist Quartet.* Cambridge: Cambridge University Press, 1994.

Monteiro, George. *Robert Frost and the New England Renaissance.* Lexington: University of Kentucky Press, 1988.

Oster, Judith. *Toward Robert Frost: The Reader and the Poet.* Athens, Georgia: University of Georgia Press, 1991.

Pack, Robert. *Belief and Uncertainty in the Poetry of Robert Frost.* Hanover: The University of New England Press, 2003.

Parini, Jay. *Robert Frost: A Life.* New York: Henry Holt, 1999.

Poirier, Richard. *Robert Frost and the Work of Knowing.* Oxford: Oxford University Press, 1977.

Pritchard, William. *Robert Frost: A Literary Life Reconsidered.* Amherst: University of Massachusetts Press, 1986.

Richardson, Mark. *The Ordeal of Robert Frost.* Urbana: University of Illinois Press, 1997.

Sheehy, Donald. *Poems, Life, Legacy.* (CD-ROM) New York: Henry Holt, 1997.

Tuten, Nancy, and John Zubizarreta, eds. *The Robert Frost Encylopedia.* Westport: Greenwood Press, 2000.

Walsh, John Evangelist. *Into My Own: The English Years of Robert Frost, 1912–1915.* New York: Grove Press, 1988.

Wilcox, Earl, ed. *Robert Frost: His Incalculable Influence on Others.* Victoria: University of Victoria, 1994.

A NOTE ON
THE TEXTS

The texts presented here are those of the first editions of *A Boy's Will*, *North of Boston*, and *Mountain Interval*. The texts of the poems Frost later included in *New Hampshire* follow their first printings.

A BOY'S WILL [1]

TO
E. M. F.

INTO MY OWN

One of my wishes is that those dark trees,
So old and firm they scarcely show the breeze,
Were not, as 'twere, the merest mask of gloom,
But stretched away unto the edge of doom.[2]

5   I should not be withheld but that some day
Into their vastness I should steal away,
Fearless of ever finding open land,
Or highway where the slow wheel pours the sand.

I do not see why I should e'er turn back,
10 Or those should not set forth upon my track
To overtake me, who should miss me here
And long to know if still I held them dear.

They would not find me changed from him they knew—
Only more sure of all I thought was true.

GHOST HOUSE

I dwell in a lonely house I know
That vanished many a summer ago,
    And left no trace but the cellar walls,
    And a cellar in which the daylight falls,
5 And the purple-stemmed wild raspberries grow.

O'er ruined fences the grape-vines shield
The woods come back to the mowing field;
    The orchard tree has grown one copse
    Of new wood and old where the woodpecker chops;
10 The footpath down to the well is healed.

I dwell with a strangely aching heart
In that vanished abode there far apart
    On that disused and forgotten road
    That has no dust-bath now for the toad.
15 Night comes; the black bats tumble and dart;

The whippoorwill is coming to shout
And hush and cluck and flutter about:
    I hear him begin far enough away
    Full many a time to say his say
20 Before he arrives to say it out.

It is under the small, dim, summer star,
I know not who these mute folk are
    Who share the unlit place with me—
    Those stones out under the low-limbed tree
25 Doubtless bear names that the mosses mar.

They are tireless folk, but slow and sad,
Though two, close-keeping, are lass and lad,—
     With none among them that ever sings,
     And yet, in view of how many things,
30   As sweet companions as might be had.

My November Guest

My Sorrow, when she's here with me,
    Thinks these dark days of autumn rain
Are beautiful as days can be;
She loves the bare, the withered tree;
5   She walks the sodden pasture lane.

Her pleasure will not let me stay.
    She talks and I am fain to list:
She's glad the birds are gone away,
She's glad her simple worsted grey
10   Is silver now with clinging mist.

The desolate, deserted trees,
    The faded earth, the heavy sky,
The beauties she so truly sees,
She thinks I have no eye for these,
15   And vexes me for reason why.

Not yesterday I learned to know
    The love of bare November days
Before the coming of the snow,
But it were vain to tell her so,
20   And they are better for her praise.

Love and a Question

A stranger came to the door at eve,
   And he spoke the bridegroom fair.
He bore a green-white stick in his hand,
   And, for all burden, care.
5 He asked with the eyes more than the lips
   For a shelter for the night,
And he turned and looked at the road afar
   Without a window light.

The bridegroom came forth into the porch
10   With "Let us look at the sky,
And question what of the night to be,
   Stranger, you and I."
The woodbine leaves littered the yard,
   The woodbine berries were blue,
15 Autumn, yes, winter was in the wind;
   "Stranger, I wish I knew."

Within, the bride in the dusk alone
   Bent over the open fire,
Her face rose-red with the glowing coal
20   And the thought of the heart's desire.
The bridegroom looked at the weary road,
   Yet saw but her within,
And wished her heart in a case of gold
   And pinned with a silver pin.

25 The bridegroom thought it little to give
   A dole of bread, a purse,
A heartfelt prayer for the poor of God,
   Or for the rich a curse;

But whether or not a man was asked
30   To mar the love of two
By harboring woe in the bridal house,
    The bridegroom wished he knew.

A Late Walk

When I go up through the mowing field,
    The headless aftermath,
Smooth-laid like thatch with the heavy dew,
    Half closes the garden path.

5   And when I come to the garden ground,
    The whir of sober birds
Up from the tangle of withered weeds
    Is sadder than any words.

A tree beside the wall stands bare,
10   But a leaf that lingered brown,
Disturbed, I doubt not, by my thought,
    Comes softly rattling down.

I end not far from my going forth
    By picking the faded blue
15 Of the last remaining aster flower
    To carry again to you.

STARS

How countlessly they congregate
   O'er our tumultuous snow,
Which flows in shapes as tall as trees
   When wintry winds do blow!—

5 As if with keenness for our fate,
   Our faltering few steps on
To white rest, and a place of rest
   Invisible at dawn,—

And yet with neither love nor hate,
10   Those stars like some snow-white
Minerva's snow-white marble eyes
   Without the gift of sight.

STORM FEAR

When the wind works against us in the dark,
And pelts with snow
The lower chamber window on the east,
And whispers with a sort of stifled bark,
5   The beast,
"Come out! Come out!"—
It costs no inward struggle not to go,
Ah, no!
I count our strength,
10   Two and a child,
Those of us not asleep subdued to mark
How the cold creeps as the fire dies at length,—
How drifts are piled,
Dooryard and road ungraded,
15   Till even the comforting barn grows far away
And my heart owns a doubt
Whether 'tis in us to arise with day
And save ourselves unaided.

Wind and Window Flower

Lovers, forget your love,
    And list to the love of these,
She a window flower,
    And he a winter breeze.

5 When the frosty window veil
    Was melted down at noon,
And the caged yellow bird
    Hung over her in tune,

He marked her through the pane,
10   He could not help but mark,
And only passed her by,
    To come again at dark.

He was a winter wind,
    Concerned with ice and snow,
15 Dead weeds and unmated birds,
    And little of love could know.

But he sighed upon the sill,
    He gave the sash a shake,
As witness all within
20   Who lay that night awake.

Perchance he half prevailed
    To win her for the flight
From the firelit looking-glass
    And warm stove-window light.

25   But the flower leaned aside
       And thought of naught to say,
    And morning found the breeze
       A hundred miles away.

To the Thawing Wind

Come with rain, O loud Southwester!
Bring the singer, bring the nester;
Give the buried flower a dream;
Make the settled snow-bank steam;
5   Find the brown beneath the white;
But whate'er you do to-night,
Bathe my window, make it flow,
Melt it as the ices go;
Melt the glass and leave the sticks
10   Like a hermit's crucifix;
Burst into my narrow stall;
Swing the picture on the wall;
Run the rattling pages o'er;
Scatter poems on the floor;
15   Turn the poet out of door.

A Prayer in Spring

Oh, give us pleasure in the flowers to-day;
And give us not to think so far away
As the uncertain harvest; keep us here
All simply in the springing of the year.

5   Oh, give us pleasure in the orchard white,
Like nothing else by day, like ghosts by night;
And make us happy in the happy bees,
The swarm dilating round the perfect trees.

And make us happy in the darting bird
10 That suddenly above the bees is heard,
The meteor that thrusts in with needle bill,
And off a blossom in mid air stands still.

For this is love and nothing else is love,
The which it is reserved for God above
15 To sanctify to what far ends He will,
But which it only needs that we fulfil.

FLOWER-GATHERING

I left you in the morning,
And in the morning glow,
You walked a way beside me
To make me sad to go.
5   Do you know me in the gloaming,
Gaunt and dusty grey with roaming?
Are you dumb because you know me not,
Or dumb because you know?

All for me? And not a question
10   For the faded flowers gay
That could take me from beside you
For the ages of a day?
They are yours, and be the measure
Of their worth for you to treasure,
15   The measure of the little while
That I've been long away.

ROSE POGONIAS[3]

A saturated meadow,
    Sun-shaped and jewel-small,
A circle scarcely wider
    Than the trees around were tall;
5   Where winds were quite excluded,
    And the air was stifling sweet
With the breath of many flowers,—
    A temple of the heat.

There we bowed us in the burning,
10   As the sun's right worship is,
To pick where none could miss them
    A thousand orchises;
For though the grass was scattered,
    Yet every second spear
15   Seemed tipped with wings of color,
    That tinged the atmosphere.

We raised a simple prayer
    Before we left the spot,
That in the general mowing
20   That place might be forgot;
Or if not all so favoured,
    Obtain such grace of hours,
That none should mow the grass there
    While so confused with flowers.

ASKING FOR ROSES

A house that lacks, seemingly, mistress and master,
　　With doors that none but the wind ever closes,
Its floor all littered with glass and with plaster;
　　It stands in a garden of old-fashioned roses.

5　I pass by that way in the gloaming with Mary;
　　　"I wonder," I say, "who the owner of those is."
"Oh, no one you know," she answers me airy,
　　"But one we must ask if we want any roses."

So we must join hands in the dew coming coldly
10　　There in the hush of the wood that reposes,
And turn and go up to the open door boldly,
　　And knock to the echoes as beggars for roses.

"Pray, are you within there, Mistress Who-were-you?"
　　'Tis Mary that speaks and our errand discloses.
15　"Pray, are you within there? Bestir you, bestir you!
　　'Tis summer again; there's two come for roses.

"A word with you, that of the singer recalling—
　　Old Herrick: a saying that every maid knows is
A flower unplucked is but left to the falling,
20　　And nothing is gained by not gathering roses."

We do not loosen our hands' intertwining
　　(Not caring so very much what she supposes),
There when she comes on us mistily shining
　　And grants us by silence the boon of her roses.

WAITING
Afield at Dusk

What things for dream there are when spectre-like,
Moving among tall haycocks lightly piled,
I enter alone upon the stubble field,
From which the laborers' voices late have died,
And in the antiphony of afterglow
And rising full moon, sit me down
Upon the full moon's side of the first haycock
And lose myself amid so many alike.

I dream upon the opposing lights of the hour,
Preventing shadow until the moon prevail;
I dream upon the night-hawks peopling heaven,
Each circling each with vague unearthly cry,
Or plunging headlong with fierce twang afar;
And on the bat's mute antics, who would seem
Dimly to have made out my secret place,
Only to lose it when he pirouettes,
And seek it endlessly with purblind haste;
On the last swallow's sweep; and on the rasp
In the abyss of odor and rustle at my back,
That, silenced by my advent, finds once more,
After an interval, his instrument,
And tries once—twice—and thrice if I be there;
And on the worn book of old-golden song[4]
I brought not here to read, it seems, but hold
And freshen in this air of withering sweetness;
But on the memory of one absent most,
For whom these lines when they shall greet her eye.

In a Vale

When I was young, we dwelt in a vale
   By a misty fen that rang all night,
And thus it was the maidens pale
I knew so well, whose garments trail
5   Across the reeds to a window light.

The fen had every kind of bloom,
   And for every kind there was a face,
And a voice that has sounded in my room
Across the sill from the outer gloom.
10   Each came singly unto her place,

But all came every night with the mist;
   And often they brought so much to say
Of things of moment to which, they wist,
One so lonely was fain to list,
15   That the stars were almost faded away

Before the last went, heavy with dew,
   Back to the place from which she came—
Where the bird was before it flew,
Where the flower was before it grew,
20   Where bird and flower were one and the same.

And thus it is I know so well
   Why the flower has odor, the bird has song.
You have only to ask me, and I can tell.
No, not vainly there did I dwell,
25   Nor vainly listen all the night long.

A Dream Pang

I had withdrawn in forest, and my song
Was swallowed up in leaves that blew alway;
And to the forest edge you came one day
(This was my dream) and looked and pondered long,
5   But did not enter, though the wish was strong:
You shook your pensive head as who should say,
"I dare not—too far in his footsteps stray—
He must seek me would he undo the wrong."

Not far, but near, I stood and saw it all
10 Behind low boughs the trees let down outside;
And the sweet pang it cost me not to call
And tell you that I saw does still abide.
But 'tis not true that thus I dwelt aloof,
For the wood wakes, and you are here for proof.

In Neglect

They leave us so to the way we took,
　　As two in whom they were proved mistaken,
That we sit sometimes in the wayside nook,
With mischievous, vagrant, seraphic look,
5　　And *try* if we cannot feel forsaken.

THE VANTAGE POINT

If tired of trees I seek again mankind,
    Well I know where to hie me—in the dawn,
    To a slope where the cattle keep the lawn.
There amid lolling juniper reclined,
5 Myself unseen, I see in white defined
    Far off the homes of men, and farther still,
    The graves of men on an opposing hill,
Living or dead, whichever are to mind.

And if by noon I have too much of these,
10   I have but to turn on my arm, and lo,
    The sun-burned hillside sets my face aglow,
My breathing shakes the bluet like a breeze,
    I smell the earth, I smell the bruised plant,
    I look into the crater of the ant.

Mowing

There was never a sound beside the wood but one,
And that was my long scythe whispering to the ground.
What was it it whispered? I knew not well myself;
Perhaps it was something about the heat of the sun,
5   Something, perhaps, about the lack of sound—
And that was why it whispered and did not speak.
It was no dream of the gift of idle hours,
Or easy gold at the hand of fay or elf:
Anything more than the truth would have seemed too weak
10   To the earnest love that laid the swale in rows,
Not without feeble-pointed spikes of flowers
(Pale orchises), and scared a bright green snake.[5]
The fact is the sweetest dream that labor knows.
My long scythe whispered and left the hay to make.

Going for Water

The well was dry beside the door,
    And so we went with pail and can
Across the fields behind the house
    To seek the brook if still it ran;

5   Not loth to have excuse to go,
    Because the autumn eve was fair
(Though chill), because the fields were ours,
    And by the brook our woods were there.

We ran as if to meet the moon
10   That slowly dawned behind the trees,
The barren boughs without the leaves,
    Without the birds, without the breeze.

But once within the wood, we paused
    Like gnomes that hid us from the moon,
15 Ready to run to hiding new
    With laughter when she found us soon.

Each laid on other a staying hand
    To listen ere we dared to look,
And in the hush we joined to make
20   We heard, we knew we heard the brook.

A note as from a single place,
    A slender tinkling fall that made
Now drops that floated on the pool
    Like pearls, and now a silver blade.

REVELATION

We make ourselves a place apart
    Behind light words that tease and flout,
But oh, the agitated heart
    Till someone find us really out.

5 'Tis pity if the case require
    (Or so we say) that in the end
We speak the literal to inspire
    The understanding of a friend.

But so with all, from babes that play
10   At hide-and-seek to God afar,
So all who hide too well away
    Must speak and tell us where they are.

THE TRIAL BY EXISTENCE

Even the bravest that are slain
    Shall not dissemble their surprise
On waking to find valor reign,
    Even as on earth, in paradise;
5 And where they sought without the sword
    Wide fields of asphodel fore'er,[6]
To find that the utmost reward
    Of daring should be still to dare.

The light of heaven falls whole and white
10   And is not shattered into dyes,
The light for ever is morning light;
    The hills are verdured pasture-wise;
The angel hosts with freshness go,
    And seek with laughter what to brave;—
15 And binding all is the hushed snow
    Of the far-distant breaking wave.

And from a cliff-top is proclaimed
    The gathering of the souls for birth,
The trial by existence named,
20   The obscuration upon earth.
And the slant spirits trooping by
    In streams and cross- and counter-streams
Can but give ear to that sweet cry
    For its suggestion of what dreams!

25 And the more loitering are turned
    To view once more the sacrifice
Of those who for some good discerned
    Will gladly give up paradise.

And a white shimmering concourse rolls
30   Toward the throne to witness there
The speeding of devoted souls
     Which God makes his especial care.

And none are taken but who will,
     Having first heard the life read out
35 That opens earthward, good and ill,
     Beyond the shadow of a doubt;
And very beautifully God limns,
     And tenderly, life's little dream,
But naught extenuates or dims,
40   Setting the thing that is supreme.

Nor is there wanting in the press
     Some spirit to stand simply forth,
Heroic in its nakedness,
     Against the uttermost of earth.
45 The tale of earth's unhonored things
     Sounds nobler there than 'neath the sun;
And the mind whirls and the heart sings,
     And a shout greets the daring one.

But always God speaks at the end:
50   "One thought in agony of strife
The bravest would have by for friend,
     The memory that he chose the life;
But the pure fate to which you go
     Admits no memory of choice,
55 Or the woe were not earthly woe
     To which you give the assenting voice."

And so the choice must be again,
  But the last choice is still the same;
And the awe passes wonder then,
60   And a hush falls for all acclaim.
And God has taken a flower of gold
  And broken it, and used therefrom
The mystic link to bind and hold
  Spirit to matter till death come.

65 'Tis of the essence of life here,
  Though we choose greatly, still to lack
The lasting memory at all clear,
  That life has for us on the wrack
Nothing but what we somehow chose;
70   Thus are we wholly stripped of pride
In the pain that has but one close,
  Bearing it crushed and mystified.

IN EQUAL SACRIFICE

Thus of old the Douglas did:
He left his land as he was bid
With the royal heart of Robert the Bruce
In a golden case with a golden lid,

To carry the same to the Holy Land;
By which we see and understand
That that was the place to carry a heart
At loyalty and love's command,

And that was the case to carry it in.
The Douglas had not far to win
Before he came to the land of Spain,
Where long a holy war had been

Against the too-victorious Moor;
And there his courage could not endure
Not to strike a blow for God
Before he made his errand sure.

And ever it was intended so,
That a man for God should strike a blow,
No matter the heart he has in charge
For the Holy Land where hearts should go.

But when in battle the foe were met,
The Douglas found him sore beset,
With only strength of the fighting arm
For one more battle passage yet—

25 And that as vain to save the day
   As bring his body safe away—
   Only a signal deed to do
   And a last sounding word to say.

   The heart he wore in a golden chain
30 He swung and flung forth into the plain,
   And followed it crying "Heart or death!"
   And fighting over it perished fain.

   So may another do of right,
   Give a heart to the hopeless fight,
35 The more of right the more he loves;
   So may another redouble might

   For a few swift gleams of the angry brand,
   Scorning greatly not to demand
   In equal sacrifice with his
40 The heart he bore to the Holy Land.

The Tuft of Flowers

I went to turn the grass once after one
Who mowed it in the dew before the sun.

The dew was gone that made his blade so keen
Before I came to view the levelled scene.

5   I looked for him behind an isle of trees;
I listened for his whetstone on the breeze.

But he had gone his way, the grass all mown,
And I must be, as he had been,—alone,

"As all must be," I said within my heart,
10 "Whether they work together or apart."

But as I said it, swift there passed me by
On noiseless wing a 'wildered butterfly,

Seeking with memories grown dim o'er night
Some resting flower of yesterday's delight.

15 And once I marked his flight go round and round,
As where some flower lay withering on the ground.

And then he flew as far as eye could see,
And then on tremulous wing came back to me.

I thought of questions that have no reply,
20 And would have turned to toss the grass to dry;

But he turned first, and led my eye to look
At a tall tuft of flowers beside a brook,

A leaping tongue of bloom the scythe had spared
Beside a reedy brook the scythe had bared.

25 I left my place to know them by their name,
Finding them butterfly weed when I came.

The mower in the dew had loved them thus,
By leaving them to flourish, not for us,

Nor yet to draw one thought of ours to him.
30 But from sheer morning gladness at the brim.

The butterfly and I had lit upon,
Nevertheless, a message from the dawn,

That made me hear the wakening birds around,
And hear his long scythe whispering to the ground,

35 And feel a spirit kindred to my own;
So that henceforth I worked no more alone;

But glad with him, I worked as with his aid,
And weary, sought at noon with him the shade;

And dreaming, as it were, held brotherly speech
40 With one whose thought I had not hoped to reach.

"Men work together," I told him from the heart,
"Whether they work together or apart."

SPOILS OF THE DEAD

Two fairies it was
　　On a still summer day
Came forth in the woods
　　With the flowers to play.

5　The flowers they plucked
　　They cast on the ground
For others, and those
　　For still others they found.

Flower-guided it was
10　　That they came as they ran
On something that lay
　　In the shape of a man.

The snow must have made
　　The feathery bed
15　When this one fell
　　On the sleep of the dead.

But the snow was gone
　　A long time ago,
And the body he wore
20　　Nigh gone with the snow.

The fairies drew near
　　And keenly espied
A ring on his hand
　　And a chain at his side.

25 They knelt in the leaves
     And eerily played
With the glittering things,
     And were not afraid.

And when they went home
30   To hide in their burrow,
They took them along
     To play with to-morrow.

When *you* came on death,
     Did you not come flower-guided
35 Like the elves in the wood?
     I remember that I did.

But I recognised death
     With sorrow and dread,
And I hated and hate
40   The spoils of the dead.

Pan with Us

Pan came out of the woods one day,—
His skin and his hair and his eyes were gray,
The gray of the moss of walls were they,—
    And stood in the sun and looked his fill
5   At wooded valley and wooded hill.

He stood in the zephyr, pipes in hand,
On a height of naked pasture land;
In all the country he did command
    He saw no smoke and he saw no roof.
10   That was well! and he stamped a hoof.

His heart knew peace, for none came here
To this lean feeding save once a year
Someone to salt the half-wild steer,
    Or homespun children with clicking pails
15   Who see so little they tell no tales.

He tossed his pipes, too hard to teach
A new-world song, far out of reach,
For a sylvan sign that the blue jay's screech
    And the whimper of hawks beside the sun
20   Were music enough for him, for one.

Times were changed from what they were:
Such pipes kept less of power to stir
The fruited bough of the juniper
    And the fragile bluets clustered there
25   Than the merest aimless breath of air.

They were pipes of pagan mirth,
And the world had found new terms of worth.
He laid him down on the sun-burned earth
    And ravelled a flower and looked away—
30   Play? Play?—What should he play?

The Demiurge's Laugh[7]

It was far in the sameness of the wood;
  I was running with joy on the Demon's trail,
Though I knew what I hunted was no true god.
  It was just as the light was beginning to fail
5 That I suddenly heard—all I needed to hear:
It has lasted me many and many a year.

The sound was behind me instead of before,
  A sleepy sound, but mocking half,
As of one who utterly couldn't care.
10   The Demon arose from his wallow to laugh,
Brushing the dirt from his eye as he went;
And well I knew what the Demon meant.

I shall not forget how his laugh rang out.
  I felt as a fool to have been so caught,
15 And checked my steps to make pretence
  It was something among the leaves I sought
(Though doubtful whether he stayed to see).
Thereafter I sat me against a tree.

Now Close the Windows

Now close the windows and hush all the fields;
    If the trees must, let them silently toss;
No bird is singing now, and if there is,
    Be it my loss.

5 It will be long ere the marshes resume,
    It will be long ere the earliest bird:
So close the windows and not hear the wind,
    But see all wind-stirred.

A Line-Storm Song

The line-storm clouds fly tattered and swift,
　　The road is forlorn all day,
Where a myriad snowy quartz stones lift,
　　And the hoof-prints vanish away.
5　The roadside flowers, too wet for the bee,
　　Expend their bloom in vain.
Come over the hills and far with me,
　　And be my love in the rain.

The birds have less to say for themselves
10　　In the wood-world's torn despair
Than now these numberless years the elves,
　　Although they are no less there:
All song of the woods is crushed like some
　　Wild, easily shattered rose.
15　Come, be my love in the wet woods; come,
　　Where the boughs rain when it blows.

There is the gale to urge behind
　　And bruit our singing down,
And the shallow waters aflutter with wind
20　　From which to gather your gown.
What matter if we go clear to the west,
　　And come not through dry-shod?
For wilding brooch shall wet your breast
　　The rain-fresh goldenrod.

25　Oh, never this whelming east wind swells
　　But it seems like the sea's return
To the ancient lands where it left the shells
　　Before the age of the fern;

And it seems like the time when after doubt
Our love came back amain.
Oh, come forth into the storm and rout
And be my love in the rain.

OCTOBER

O hushed October morning mild,
Thy leaves have ripened to the fall;
To-morrow's wind, if it be wild,
Should waste them all.
5 The crows above the forest call;
To-morrow they may form and go.
O hushed October morning mild,
Begin the hours of this day slow,
Make the day seem to us less brief.
10 Hearts not averse to being beguiled,
Beguile us in the way you know;
Release one leaf at break of day;
At noon release another leaf;
One from our trees, one far away;
15 Retard the sun with gentle mist;
Enchant the land with amethyst.
Slow, slow!
For the grapes' sake, if they were all,
Whose leaves already are burnt with frost,
20 Whose clustered fruit must else be lost—
For the grapes' sake along the wall.

My Butterfly

Thine emulous fond flowers are dead, too,
And the daft sun-assaulter, he
That frighted thee so oft, is fled or dead:
Save only me
5   (Nor is it sad to thee!)
Save only me
There is none left to mourn thee in the fields.

The gray grass is not dappled with the snow;
Its two banks have not shut upon the river;
10 But it is long ago—
It seems forever—
Since first I saw thee glance,
With all the dazzling other ones,
In airy dalliance,
15 Precipitate in love,
Tossed, tangled, whirled and whirled above,
Like a limp rose-wreath in a fairy dance.

When that was, the soft mist
Of my regret hung not on all the land,
20 And I was glad for thee,
And glad for me, I wist.

Thou didst not know, who tottered, wandering on high,
That fate had made thee for the pleasure of the wind,
With those great careless wings,
25 Nor yet did I.

And there were other things:
It seemed God let thee flutter from his gentle clasp:
Then fearful he had let thee win

Too far beyond him to be gathered in,
30 Snatched thee, o'er eager, with ungentle grasp.

Ah! I remember me
How once conspiracy was rife
Against my life—
The languor of it and the dreaming fond;
35 Surging, the grasses dizzied me of thought,
The breeze three odors brought,
And a gem-flower waved in a wand!

Then when I was distraught
And could not speak,
40 Sidelong, full on my cheek,
What should that reckless zephyr fling
But the wild touch of thy dye-dusty wing!

I found that wing broken to-day!
For thou art dead, I said,
45 And the strange birds say.
I found it with the withered leaves
Under the eaves.

RELUCTANCE

Out through the fields and the woods
    And over the walls I have wended;
I have climbed the hills of view
    And looked at the world, and descended;
5 I have come by the highway home,
    And lo, it is ended.

The leaves are all dead on the ground,
    Save those that the oak is keeping
To ravel them one by one
10   And let them go scraping and creeping
Out over the crusted snow,
    When others are sleeping.

And the dead leaves lie huddled and still,
    No longer blown hither and thither;
15 The last lone aster is gone;
    The flowers of the witch-hazel wither;
The heart is still aching to seek,
    But the feet question "Whither?"

Ah, when to the heart of man
20   Was it ever less than a treason
To go with the drift of things,
    To yield with a grace to reason,
And bow and accept the end
    Of a love or a season?

NORTH OF BOSTON [8]

THE PASTURE

I'm going out to clean the pasture spring;
I'll only stop to rake the leaves away
(And wait to watch the water clear, I may):
I sha'n't be gone long.—You come too.

5   I'm going out to fetch the little calf
That's standing by the mother. It's so young,
It totters when she licks it with her tongue.
I sha'n't be gone long.—You come too.

"Mending Wall" takes up the theme where
"A Tuft of Flowers" in *A Boy's Will*
laid it down.

Mending Wall[9]

Something there is that doesn't love a wall,
That sends the frozen-ground-swell under it,
And spills the upper boulders in the sun;
And makes gaps even two can pass abreast.
5 The work of hunters is another thing:
I have come after them and made repair
Where they have left not one stone on stone,
But they would have the rabbit out of hiding,
To please the yelping dogs. The gaps I mean,
10 No one has seen them made or heard them made,
But at spring mending-time we find them there.
I let my neighbour know beyond the hill;
And on a day we meet to walk the line
And set the wall between us once again.
15 We keep the wall between us as we go.
To each the boulders that have fallen to each.
And some are loaves and some so nearly balls
We have to use a spell to make them balance:
"Stay where you are until our backs are turned!"
20 We wear our fingers rough with handling them.
Oh, just another kind of out-door game,
One on a side. It comes to little more:
There where it is we do not need the wall:
He is all pine and I am apple orchard.
25 My apple trees will never get across
And eat the cones under his pines, I tell him.
He only says, "Good fences make good neighbours."
Spring is the mischief in me, and I wonder
If I could put a notion in his head:
30 "*Why* do they make good neighbours? Isn't it
Where there are cows? But here there are no cows.
Before I built a wall I'd ask to know

What I was walling in or walling out,
And to whom I was like to give offence.
35 Something there is that doesn't love a wall,
That wants it down." I could say "Elves" to him,
But it's not elves exactly, and I'd rather
He said it for himself. I see him there
Bringing a stone grasped firmly by the top
40 In each hand, like an old-stone savage armed.
He moves in darkness as it seems to me,
Not of woods only and the shade of trees.
He will not go behind his father's saying,
And he likes having thought of it so well
45 He says again, "Good fences make good neighbours."

THE DEATH OF THE HIRED MAN

Mary sat musing on the lamp-flame at the table
Waiting for Warren. When she heard his step,
She ran on tip-toe down the darkened passage
To meet him in the doorway with the news

5   And put him on his guard. "Silas is back."
She pushed him outward with her through the door
And shut it after her. "Be kind," she said.
She took the market things from Warren's arms
And set them on the porch, then drew him down

10 To sit beside her on the wooden steps.

"When was I ever anything but kind to him?
But I'll not have the fellow back," he said.
"I told him so last haying, didn't I?
If he left then, I said, that ended it.

15 What good is he? Who else will harbour him
At his age for the little he can do?
What help he is there's no depending on.
Off he goes always when I need him most.
He thinks he ought to earn a little pay,

20 Enough at least to buy tobacco with,
So he won't have to beg and be beholden.
'All right,' I say, 'I can't afford to pay
Any fixed wages, though I wish I could.'
'Someone else can.' 'Then someone else will have to.'

25 I shouldn't mind his bettering himself
If that was what it was. You can be certain,
When he begins like that, there's someone at him
Trying to coax him off with pocket-money,—
In haying time, when any help is scarce.

30 In winter he comes back to us. I'm done."

"Sh! not so loud: he'll hear you," Mary said.

"I want him to: he'll have to soon or late."

"He's worn out. He's asleep beside the stove.
When I came up from Rowe's I found him here,
35 Huddled against the barn-door fast asleep,
A miserable sight, and frightening, too—
You needn't smile—I didn't recognise him—
I wasn't looking for him—and he's changed.
Wait till you see."

            "Where did you say he'd been?"

40 "He didn't say. I dragged him to the house,
And gave him tea and tried to make him smoke.
I tried to make him talk about his travels.
Nothing would do: he just kept nodding off."

"What did he say? Did he say anything?"

45 "But little."

          "Anything? Mary, confess
He said he'd come to ditch the meadow for me."

"Warren!"

        "But did he? I just want to know."

"Of course he did. What would you have him say?
Surely you wouldn't grudge the poor old man

50 Some humble way to save his self-respect.
He added, if you really care to know,
He meant to clear the upper pasture, too.
That sounds like something you have heard before?
Warren, I wish you could have heard the way
55 He jumbled everything. I stopped to look
Two or three times—he made me feel so queer—
To see if he was talking in his sleep.
He ran on Harold Wilson—you remember—
The boy you had in haying four years since.
60 He's finished school, and teaching in his college.
Silas declares you'll have to get him back.
He says they two will make a team for work:
Between them they will lay this farm as smooth!
The way he mixed that in with other things.
65 He thinks young Wilson a likely lad, though daft
On education—you know how they fought
All through July under the blazing sun,
Silas up on the cart to build the load,
Harold along beside to pitch it on."

70 "Yes, I took care to keep well out of earshot."

"Well, those days trouble Silas like a dream.
You wouldn't think they would. How some things linger!
Harold's young college boy's assurance piqued him.
After so many years he still keeps finding
75 Good arguments he sees he might have used.
I sympathise. I know just how it feels
To think of the right thing to say too late.
Harold's associated in his mind with Latin.
He asked me what I thought of Harold's saying

- 55 -

80 He studied Latin like the violin
    Because he liked it—that an argument!
    He said he couldn't make the boy believe
    He could find water with a hazel prong—
    Which showed how much good school had ever done him.
85 He wanted to go over that. But most of all
    He thinks if he could have another chance
    To teach him how to build a load of hay——"

    "I know, that's Silas' one accomplishment.
    He bundles every forkful in its place,
90 And tags and numbers it for future reference,
    So he can find and easily dislodge it
    In the unloading. Silas does that well.
    He takes it out in bunches like big birds' nests.
    You never see him standing on the hay
95 He's trying to lift, straining to lift himself."

    "He thinks if he could teach him that, he'd be
    Some good perhaps to someone in the world.
    He hates to see a boy the fool of books.
    Poor Silas, so concerned for other folk,
100 And nothing to look backward to with pride,
    And nothing to look forward to with hope,
    So now and never any different."

    Part of a moon was falling down the west,
    Dragging the whole sky with it to the hills.
105 Its light poured softly in her lap. She saw
    And spread her apron to it. She put out her hand
    Among the harp-like morning-glory strings,
    Taut with the dew from garden bed to eaves,

As if she played unheard the tenderness
110 That wrought on him beside her in the night.
"Warren," she said, "he has come home to die:
You needn't be afraid he'll leave you this time."

"Home," he mocked gently.

                        "Yes, what else but home?
It all depends on what you mean by home.
115 Of course he's nothing to us, any more
Than was the hound that came a stranger to us
Out of the woods, worn out upon the trail."

"Home is the place where, when you have to go there,
They have to take you in."

                       "I should have called it
120 Something you somehow haven't to deserve."

Warren leaned out and took a step or two,
Picked up a little stick, and brought it back
And broke it in his hand and tossed it by.
"Silas has better claim on us you think
125 Than on his brother? Thirteen little miles
As the road winds would bring him to his door.
Silas has walked that far no doubt to-day.
Why didn't he go there? His brother's rich,
A somebody—director in the bank."

130 "He never told us that."

                       "We know it though."

"I think his brother ought to help, of course.
I'll see to that if there is need. He ought of right
To take him in, and might be willing to—
He may be better than appearances.
135 But have some pity on Silas. Do you think
If he'd had any pride in claiming kin
Or anything he looked for from his brother,
He'd keep so still about him all this time?"

"I wonder what's between them."

                              "I can tell you.
140 Silas is what he is—we wouldn't mind him—
But just the kind that kinsfolk can't abide.
He never did a thing so very bad.
He don't know why he isn't quite as good
As anyone. He won't be made ashamed
145 To please his brother, worthless though he is."

"*I* can't think Si ever hurt anyone."

"No, but he hurt my heart the way he lay
And rolled his old head on that sharp-edged chair-back.
He wouldn't let me put him on the lounge.
150 You must go in and see what you can do.
I made the bed up for him there to-night.
You'll be surprised at him—how much he's broken.
His working days are done; I'm sure of it."

"I'd not be in a hurry to say that."

155 "I haven't been. Go, look, see for yourself.
But, Warren, please remember how it is:
He's come to help you ditch the meadow.
He has a plan. You mustn't laugh at him.
He may not speak of it, and then he may.
160 I'll sit and see if that small sailing cloud
Will hit or miss the moon."

It hit the moon.
Then there were three there, making a dim row,
The moon, the little silver cloud, and she.

Warren returned—too soon, it seemed to her,
165 Slipped to her side, caught up her hand and waited.

"Warren," she questioned.

"Dead," was all he answered.

The Mountain

The mountain held the town as in a shadow
I saw so much before I slept there once:
I noticed that I missed stars in the west,
Where its black body cut into the sky.
5   Near me it seemed: I felt it like a wall
Behind which I was sheltered from a wind.
And yet between the town and it I found,
When I walked forth at dawn to see new things,
Were fields, a river, and beyond, more fields.
10   The river at the time was fallen away,
And made a widespread brawl on cobble-stones;
But the signs showed what it had done in spring;
Good grass-land gullied out, and in the grass
Ridges of sand, and driftwood stripped of bark.
15   I crossed the river and swung round the mountain.
And there I met a man who moved so slow
With white-faced oxen in a heavy cart,
It seemed no harm to stop him altogether.

"What town is this?" I asked.

                                 "This? Lunenburg."

20   Then I was wrong: the town of my sojourn,
Beyond the bridge, was not that of the mountain,
But only felt at night its shadowy presence.
"Where is your village? Very far from here?"

"There is no village—only scattered farms.
25   We were but sixty voters last election.
We can't in nature grow to many more:

That thing takes all the room!" He moved his goad.
The mountain stood there to be pointed at.
Pasture ran up the side a little way,
30   And then there was a wall of trees with trunks:
After that only tops of trees, and cliffs
Imperfectly concealed among the leaves.
A dry ravine emerged from under boughs
Into the pasture.

                    "That looks like a path.
35   Is that the way to reach the top from here?—
Not for this morning, but some other time:
I must be getting back to breakfast now."

"I don't advise your trying from this side.
There is no proper path, but those that *have*
40   Been up, I understand, have climbed from Ladd's.
That's five miles back. You can't mistake the place:
They logged it there last winter some way up.
I'd take you, but I'm bound the other way."

"You've never climbed it?"

                              "I've been on the sides
45   Deer-hunting and trout-fishing. There's a brook
That starts up on it somewhere—I've heard say
Right on the top, tip-top—a curious thing.
But what would interest you about the brook,
It's always cold in summer, warm in winter.
50   One of the great sights going is to see
It steam in winter like an ox's breath,

Until the bushes all along its banks
Are inch-deep with the frosty spines and bristles—
You know the kind. Then let the sun shine on it!"

55 "There ought to be a view around the world
From such a mountain—if it isn't wooded
Clear to the top." I saw through leafy screens
Great granite terraces in sun and shadow,
Shelves one could rest a knee on getting up—
60 With depths behind him sheer a hundred feet;
Or turn and sit on and look out and down,
With little ferns in crevices at his elbow.

"As to that I can't say. But there's the spring,
Right on the summit, almost like a fountain.
65 That ought to be worth seeing."

                              "If it's there.
You never saw it?"

                    "I guess there's no doubt
About its being there. I never saw it.
It may not be right on the very top:
It wouldn't have to be a long way down
70 To have some head of water from above,
And a *good distance* down might not be noticed
By anyone who'd come a long way up.
One time I asked a fellow climbing it
To look and tell me later how it was."

75 "What did he say?"

                    "He said there was a lake
Somewhere in Ireland on a mountain top."

"But a lake's different. What about the spring?"

"He never got up high enough to see.
That's why I don't advise your trying this side.
80 He tried this side. I've always meant to go
And look myself, but you know how it is:
It doesn't seem so much to climb a mountain
You've worked around the foot of all your life.
What would I do? Go in my overalls,
85 With a big stick, the same as when the cows
Haven't come down to the bars at milking time?
Or with a shotgun for a stray black bear?
'Twouldn't seem real to climb for climbing it."

"I shouldn't climb it if I didn't want to—
90 Not for the sake of climbing. What's its name?"

"We call it Hor:[10] I don't know if that's right."

"Can one walk around it? Would it be too far?"

"You can drive round and keep in Lunenburg,[11]
But it's as much as you can ever do,
95 The boundary lines keep in so close to it.
Hor is the township, and the township's Hor—
And a few houses sprinkled round the foot,
Like boulders broken off the upper cliff,
Rolled out a little farther than the rest."

100 "Warm in December, cold in June, you say?"

"I don't suppose the water's changed at all.
You and I know enough to know it's warm
Compared with cold, and cold compared with warm.
But all the fun's in how you say a thing."

105 "You've lived here all your life?"

                                    "Ever since Hor
Was no bigger than a——" What, I did not hear.
He drew the oxen toward him with light touches
Of his slim goad on nose and offside flank,
Gave them their marching orders and was moving.

A Hundred Collars

Lancaster bore him—such a little town,
Such a great man. It doesn't see him often
Of late years, though he keeps the old homestead
And sends the children down there with their mother
5   To run wild in the summer—a little wild.
Sometimes he joins them for a day or two
And sees old friends he somehow can't get near.
They meet him in the general store at night,
Pre-occupied with formidable mail,
10   Rifling a printed letter as he talks.
They seem afraid. He wouldn't have it so:
Though a great scholar, he's a democrat,
If not at heart, at least on principle.
Lately when coming up to Lancaster
15   His train being late he missed another train
And had four hours to wait at Woodsville Junction
After eleven o'clock at night. Too tired
To think of sitting such an ordeal out,
He turned to the hotel to find a bed.

20   "No room," the night clerk said. "Unless——"
Woodsville's a place of shrieks and wandering lamps
And cars that shook and rattle—and *one* hotel.

"You say 'unless.' "

                    "Unless you wouldn't mind
Sharing a room with someone else."

                                "Who is it?"

"A man."

            "So I should hope. What kind of man?"

"I know him: he's all right. A man's a man.
Separate beds of course you understand."
The night clerk blinked his eyes and dared him on.

"Who's that man sleeping in the office chair?
30 Has he had the refusal of my chance?"

"He was afraid of being robbed or murdered.
What do you say?"

           "I'll have to have a bed."

The night clerk led him up three flights of stairs
And down a narrow passage full of doors,
35 At the last one of which he knocked and entered.
"Lafe, here's a fellow wants to share your room."

"Show him this way. I'm not afraid of him.
I'm not so drunk I can't take care of myself."

The night clerk clapped a bedstead on the foot.
40 "This will be yours. Good-night," he said, and went.

"Lafe was the name, I think?"

              "Yes, *Lay*fayette.
You got it the first time. And yours?"

                               "Magoon.
Doctor Magoon."

               "A Doctor?"

                        "Well, a teacher."

"Professor Square-the-circle-till-you're-tired?
45 Hold on, there's something I don't think of now
That I had on my mind to ask the first
Man that knew anything I happened in with.
I'll ask you later—don't let me forget it."

The Doctor looked at Lafe and looked away.
50 A man? A brute. Naked above the waist,
He sat there creased and shining in the light,
Fumbling the buttons in a well-starched shirt.
"I'm moving into a size-larger shirt.
I've felt mean lately; mean's no name for it.
55 I just found what the matter was to-night:
I've been a-choking like a nursery tree
When it outgrows the wire band of its name tag.
I blamed it on the hot spell we've been having.
'Twas nothing but my foolish hanging back,
60 Not liking to own up I'd grown a size.
Number eighteen this is. What size do you wear?"

The Doctor caught his throat convulsively.
"Oh—ah—fourteen—fourteen."

                        "Fourteen! You say so!
I can remember when I wore fourteen.

65 And come to think I must have back at home
More than a hundred collars, size fourteen.
Too bad to waste them all. You ought to have them.
They're yours and welcome; let me send them to you.
What makes you stand there on one leg like that?
70 You're not much furtherer than where Kike left you.
You act as if you wished you hadn't come.
Sit down or lie down, friend; you make me nervous."

The Doctor made a subdued dash for it,
And propped himself at bay against a pillow.

75 "Not that way, with your shoes on Kike's white bed.
You can't rest that way. Let me pull your shoes off."

"Don't touch me, please—I say, don't touch me, please.
I'll not be put to bed by you, my man."

"Just as you say. Have it your own way then.
80 'My man' is it? You talk like a professor.
Speaking of who's afraid of who, however,
I'm thinking I have more to lose than you
If anything should happen to be wrong.
Who wants to cut your number fourteen throat!
85 Let's have a show down as an evidence
Of good faith. There is ninety dollars.
Come, if you're not afraid."

                              "*I'm* not afraid.
There's five: that's all I carry."

       "I can search you?
Where are you moving over to? Stay still.
90 You'd better tuck your money under you
And sleep on it the way I always do
When I'm with people I don't trust at night."

"Will you believe me if I put it there
Right on the counterpane—that I do trust you?"

95 "You'd say so, Mister Man.—I'm a collector.
My ninety isn't mine—you won't think that.
I pick it up a dollar at a time
All round the country for the *Weekly News*,
Published in Bow. You know the *Weekly News*?"

100 "Known it since I was young."

       "Then you know me.
Now we are getting on together—talking.
I'm sort of Something for it at the front.
My business is to find what people want:
They pay for it, and so they ought to have it.
105 Fairbanks, he says to me—he's editor—
Feel out the public sentiment—he says.
A good deal comes on me when all is said.
The only trouble is we disagree
In politics: I'm Vermont Democrat—
110 You know what that is, sort of double-dyed;
The *News* has always been Republican.
Fairbanks, he says to me, 'Help us this year,'
Meaning by us their ticket. 'No,' I says,

'I can't and won't. You've been in long enough:
It's time you turned around and boosted us.
You'll have to pay me more than ten a week
If I'm expected to elect Bill Taft.
I doubt if I could do it anyway.' "

"You seem to shape the paper's policy."

"You see I'm in with everybody, know 'em all.
I almost know their farms as well as they do."

"You drive around? It must be pleasant work."

"It's business, but I can't say it's not fun.
What I like best's the lay of different farms,
Coming out on them from a stretch of woods,
Or over a hill or round a sudden corner.
I like to find folks getting out in spring,
Raking the dooryard, working near the house.
Later they get out further in the fields.
Everything's shut sometimes except the barn;
The family's all away in some back meadow.
There's a hay load a-coming—when it comes.
And later still they all get driven in:
The fields are stripped to lawn, the garden patches
Stripped to bare ground, the apple trees
To whips and poles. There's nobody about.
The chimney, though, keeps up a good brisk smoking.
And I lie back and ride. I take the reins
Only when someone's coming, and the mare
Stops when she likes: I tell her when to go.
I've spoiled Jemima in more ways than one."

She's got so she turns in at every house
As if she had some sort of curvature,
No matter if I have no errand there.
145 She thinks I'm sociable. I maybe am.
It's seldom I get down except for meals, though.
Folks entertain me from the kitchen doorstep,
All in a family row down to the youngest."

"One would suppose they might not be as glad
150 To see you as you are to see them."

                           "Oh,
Because I want their dollar. I don't want
Anything they've not got. I never dun.
I'm there, and they can pay me if they like.
I go nowhere on purpose: I happen by.
155 Sorry there is no cup to give you a drink.
I drink out of the bottle—not your style.
Mayn't I offer you——?"

                           "No, no, no, thank you."

"Just as you say. Here's looking at you then.—
And now I'm leaving you a little while.
160 You'll rest easier when I'm gone, perhaps—
Lie down—let yourself go and get some sleep.
But first—let's see—what was I going to ask you?
Those collars—who shall I address them to,
Suppose you aren't awake when I come back?"

165 "Really, friend, I can't let you. You—may need them."

-71-

"Not till I shrink, when they'll be out of style."

"But really I—I have so many collars."

"I don't know who I rather would have have them.
They're only turning yellow where they are.
170 But you're the doctor as the saying is.
I'll put the light out. Don't you wait for me:
I've just begun the night. You get some sleep.
I'll knock so-fashion and peep round the door
When I come back so you'll know who it is.
175 There's nothing I'm afraid of like scared people.
I don't want you should shoot me in the head.
What am I doing carrying off this bottle?
There now, you get some sleep."

He shut the door.
The Doctor slid a little down the pillow.

He saw her from the bottom of the stairs
Before she saw him. She was starting down,
Looking back over her shoulder at some fear.
She took a doubtful step and then undid it
5 To raise herself and look again. He spoke
Advancing toward her: "What is it you see
From up there always—for I want to know."
She turned and sank upon her skirts at that,
And her face changed from terrified to dull.
10 He said to gain time: "What is it you see,"
Mounting until she cowered under him.
"I will find out now—you must tell me, dear."
She, in her place, refused him any help
With the least stiffening of her neck and silence.
15 She let him look, sure that he wouldn't see,
Blind creature; and a while he didn't see.
But at last he murmured, "Oh," and again, "Oh."

"What is it—what?" she said.

                                  "Just that I see."

"You don't," she challenged. "Tell me what it is."

20 "The wonder is I didn't see at once.
I never noticed it from here before.
I must be wonted to it—that's the reason.
The little graveyard where my people are!
So small the window frames the whole of it.
25 Not so much larger than a bedroom, is it?
There are three stones of slate and one of marble,
Broad-shouldered little slabs there in the sunlight

On the sidehill. We haven't to mind *those*.
But I understand: it is not the stones,
30 But the child's mound——"

                    "Don't, don't, don't, don't," she cried.

She withdrew shrinking from beneath his arm
That rested on the banister, and slid downstairs;
And turned on him with such a daunting look,
He said twice over before he knew himself:
35 "Can't a man speak of his own child he's lost?"

"Not you! Oh, where's my hat? Oh, I don't need it!
I must get out of here. I must get air.
I don't know rightly whether any man can."

"Amy! Don't go to someone else this time.
40 Listen to me. I won't come down the stairs."
He sat and fixed his chin between his fists.
"There's something I should like to ask you, dear."

"You don't know how to ask it."

                    "Help me, then."
Her fingers moved the latch for all reply.

45 "My words are nearly always an offence.
I don't know how to speak of anything
So as to please you. But I might be taught
I should suppose. I can't say I see how.
A man must partly give up being a man
50 With women-folk. We could have some arrangement

By which I'd bind myself to keep hands off
Anything special you're a-mind to name.
Though I don't like such things 'twixt those that love.
Two that don't love can't live together without them.
55 But two that do can't live together with them."
She moved the latch a little. "Don't—don't go.
Don't carry it to someone else this time.
Tell me about it if it's something human.
Let me into your grief. I'm not so much
60 Unlike other folks as your standing there
Apart would make me out. Give me my chance.
I do think, though, you overdo it a little.
What was it brought you up to think it the thing
To take your mother-loss of a first child
65 So inconsolably—in the face of love.
You'd think his memory might be satisfied——"

"There you go sneering now!"

                                        "I'm not, I'm not!
You make me angry. I'll come down to you.
God, what a woman! And it's come to this,
70 A man can't speak of his own child that's dead."

"You can't because you don't know how.
If you had any feelings, you that dug
With your own hand—how could you?—his little grave;
I saw you from that very window there,
75 Making the gravel leap and leap in air,
Leap up, like that, like that, and land so lightly
And roll back down the mound beside the hole.
I thought, Who is that man? I didn't know you.

And I crept down the stairs and up the stairs
80 To look again, and still your spade kept lifting.
Then you came in. I heard your rumbling voice
Out in the kitchen, and I don't know why,
But I went near to see with my own eyes.
You could sit there with the stains on your shoes
85 Of the fresh earth from your own baby's grave
And talk about your everyday concerns.
You had stood the spade up against the wall
Outside there in the entry, for I saw it."

"I shall laugh the worst laugh I ever laughed.
90 I'm cursed. God, if I don't believe I'm cursed."

"I can repeat the very words you were saying.
'Three foggy mornings and one rainy day
Will rot the best birch fence a man can build.'
Think of it, talk like that at such a time!
95 What had how long it takes a birch to rot
To do with what was in the darkened parlour.
You *couldn't* care! The nearest friends can go
With anyone to death, comes so far short
They might as well not try to go at all.
100 No, from the time when one is sick to death,
One is alone, and he dies more alone.
Friends make pretence of following to the grave,
But before one is in it, their minds are turned
And making the best of their way back to life
105 And living people, and things they understand.
But the world's evil. I won't have grief so
If I can change it. Oh, I won't, I won't!"

"There, you have said it all and you feel better.
You won't go now. You're crying. Close the door.
110 The heart's gone out of it: why keep it up.
Amy! There's someone coming down the road!"

"*You*—oh, you think the talk is all. I must go—
Somewhere out of this house. How can I make you—"

"If—you—do!" She was opening the door wider.
115 "Where do you mean to go? First tell me that.
I'll follow and bring you back by force. I *will!*—"

THE BLACK COTTAGE

We chanced in passing by that afternoon
To catch it in a sort of special picture
Among tar-banded ancient cherry trees,
Set well back from the road in rank lodged grass,
5   The little cottage we were speaking of,
A front with just a door between two windows,
Fresh painted by the shower a velvet black.
We paused, the minister and I, to look.
He made as if to hold it at arm's length
10   Or put the leaves aside that framed it in.
"Pretty," he said. "Come in. No one will care."
The path was a vague parting in the grass
That led us to a weathered window-sill.
We pressed our faces to the pane. "You see," he said,
15   "Everything's as she left it when she died.
Her sons won't sell the house or the things in it.
They say they mean to come and summer here
Where they were boys. They haven't come this year.
They live so far away—one is out west—
20   It will be hard for them to keep their word.
Anyway they won't have the place disturbed."
A buttoned hair-cloth lounge spread scrolling arms
Under a crayon portrait on the wall
Done sadly from an old daguerreotype.
25   That was the father as he went to war.
She always, when she talked about war,
Sooner or later came and leaned, half knelt
Against the lounge beside it, though I doubt
If such unlifelike lines kept power to stir
30   Anything in her after all the years.
He fell at Gettysburg or Fredricksburg,
I ought to know—it makes a difference which:

Fredricksburg wasn't Gettysburg, of course.
But what I'm getting to is how forsaken
35 A little cottage this has always seemed;
Since she went more than ever, but before—
I don't mean altogether by the lives
That had gone out of it, the father first,
Then the two sons, till she was left alone.
40 (Nothing could draw her after those two sons.
She valued the considerate neglect
She had at some cost taught them after years.)
I mean by the world's having passed it by—
As we almost got by this afternoon.
45 It always seems to me a sort of mark
To measure how far fifty years have brought us.
Why not sit down if you are in no haste?
These doorsteps seldom have a visitor.
The warping boards pull out their own old nails
50 With none to tread and put them in their place.
She had her own idea of things, the old lady.
And she liked talk. She had seen Garrison[12]
And Whittier,[13] and had her story of them.
One wasn't long in learning that she thought
55 Whatever else the Civil War was for
It wasn't just to keep the States together,
Nor just to free the slaves, though it did both.
She wouldn't have believed those ends enough
To have given outright for them all she gave.
60 Her giving somehow touched the principle
That all men are created free and equal.
And to hear her quaint phrases—so removed
From the world's view to-day of all those things.
That's a hard mystery of Jefferson's.

65 What did he mean? Of course the easy way
    Is to decide it simply isn't true.
    It may not be. I heard a fellow say so.
    But never mind, the Welshman got it planted[14]
    Where it will trouble us a thousand years.
70 Each age will have to reconsider it.
    You couldn't tell her what the West was saying,
    And what the South to her serene belief.
    She had some art of hearing and yet not
    Hearing the latter wisdom of the world.
75 White was the only race she ever knew.
    Black she had scarcely seen, and yellow never.
    But how could they be made so very unlike
    By the same hand working in the same stuff?
    She had supposed the war decided that.
80 What are you going to do with such a person?
    Strange how such innocence gets its own way.
    I shouldn't be surprised if in this world
    It were the force that would at last prevail.
    Do you know but for her there was a time
85 When to please younger members of the church,
    Or rather say non-members in the church,
    Whom we all have to think of nowadays,
    I would have changed the Creed a very little?
    Not that she ever had to ask me not to;
90 It never got so far as that; but the bare thought
    Of her old tremulous bonnet in the pew,
    And of her half asleep was too much for me.
    Why, I might wake her up and startle her.
    It was the words 'descended into Hades'[15]
95 That seemed too pagan to our liberal youth.
    You know they suffered from a general onslaught.

And well, if they weren't true why keep right on
Saying them like the heathen? We could drop them.
Only—there was the bonnet in the pew.
100 Such a phrase couldn't have meant much to her.
But suppose she had missed it from the Creed
As a child misses the unsaid Good-night,
And falls asleep with heartache—how should *I* feel?
I'm just as glad she made me keep hands off,
105 For, dear me, why abandon a belief
Merely because it ceases to be true.
Cling to it long enough, and not a doubt
It will turn true again, for so it goes.
Most of the change we think we see in life
110 Is due to truths being in and out of favour.
As I sit here, and often times, I wish
I could be monarch of a desert land
I could devote and dedicate forever
To the truths we keep coming back and back to.
115 So desert it would have to be, so walled
By mountain ranges half in summer snow,
No one would covet it or think it worth
The pains of conquering to force change on.
Scattered oases where men dwelt, but mostly
120 Sand dunes held loosely in tamarisk
Blown over and over themselves in idleness.
Sand grains should sugar in the natal dew
The babe born to the desert, the sand storm
Retard mid-waste my cowering caravans—

125 "There are bees in this wall." He struck the clapboards,
Fierce heads looked out; small bodies pivoted.
We rose to go. Sunset blazed on the windows.

BLUEBERRIES

"You ought to have seen what I saw on my way
To the village, through Mortenson's pasture to-day:
Blueberries as big as the end of your thumb,
Real sky-blue, and heavy, and ready to drum
5 In the cavernous pail of the first one to come!
And all ripe together, not some of them green
And some of them ripe! You ought to have seen!"

"I don't know what part of the pasture you mean."

"You know where they cut off the woods—let me see—
10 It was two years ago—or no!—can it be
No longer than that?—and the following fall
The fire ran and burned it all up but the wall."

"Why, there hasn't been time for the bushes to grow.
That's always the way with the blueberries, though:
15 There may not have been the ghost of a sign
Of them anywhere under the shade of the pine,
But get the pine out of the way, you may burn
The pasture all over until not a fern
Or grass-blade is left, not to mention a stick,
20 And presto, they're up all around you as thick
And hard to explain as a conjuror's trick."

"It must be on charcoal they fatten their fruit.
I taste in them sometimes the flavour of soot.
And after all really they're ebony skinned:
25 The blue's but a mist from the breath of the wind,
A tarnish that goes at a touch of the hand,
And less than the tan with which pickers are tanned."

"Does Mortenson know what he has, do you think?"

"He may and not care and so leave the chewink[16]
30 To gather them for him—you know what he is.
He won't make the fact that they're rightfully his
An excuse for keeping us other folk out."

"I wonder you didn't see Loren about."

"The best of it was that I did. Do you know,
35 I was just getting through what the field had to show
And over the wall and into the road,
When who should come by, with a democrat-load
Of all the young chattering Lorens alive,
But Loren, the fatherly, out for a drive."

40 "He saw you, then? What did he do? Did he frown?"

"He just kept nodding his head up and down.
You know how politely he always goes by.
But he thought a big thought—I could tell by his eye—
Which being expressed, might be this in effect:
45 'I have left those there berries, I shrewdly suspect,
To ripen too long. I am greatly to blame.' "

"He's a thriftier person than some I could name."

"He seems to be thrifty; and hasn't he need,
With the mouths of all those young Lorens to feed?
50 He has brought them all up on wild berries, they say,
Like birds. They store a great many away.
They eat them the year round, and those they don't eat
They sell in the store and buy shoes for their feet."

"Who cares what they say? It's a nice way to live,
55 Just taking what Nature is willing to give,
Not forcing her hand with harrow and plow.
I wish you had seen his perpetual bow—
And the air of the youngsters! Not one of them turned,
And they looked so solemn-absurdly concerned.

60 "I wish I knew half what the flock of them know
Of where all the berries and other things grow,
Cranberries in bogs and raspberries on top
Of the boulder-strewn mountain, and when they will crop.
I met them one day and each had a flower
65 Stuck into his berries as fresh as a shower;
Some strange kind—they told me it hadn't a name.

"I've told you how once not long after we came,
I almost provoked poor Loren to mirth
By going to him of all people on earth
70 To ask if he knew any fruit to be had
For the picking. The rascal, he said he'd be glad
To tell if he knew. But the year had been bad.
There *had* been some berries—but those were all gone.
He didn't say where they had been. He went on:
75 'I'm sure—I'm sure'—as polite as could be.
He spoke to his wife in the door, 'Let me see,
Mame, *we* don't know any good berrying place?'
It was all he could do to keep a straight face.

"If he thinks all the fruit that grows wild is for him,
80 He'll find he's mistaken. See here, for a whim,
We'll pick in the Mortensons' pasture this year.
We'll go in the morning, that is, if it's clear,

And the sun shines out warm: the vines must be wet.
It's so long since I picked I almost forget
85   How we used to pick berries: we took one look round,
Then sank out of sight like trolls underground,
And saw nothing more of each other, or heard,
Unless when you said I was keeping a bird
Away from its nest, and I said it was you.
90   'Well, one of us is.' For complaining it flew
Around and around us. And then for a while
We picked, till I feared you had wandered a mile,
And I thought I had lost you. I lifted a shout
Too loud for the distance you were, it turned out,
95   For when you made answer, your voice was as low
As talking—you stood up beside me, you know.

"We shan't have the place to ourselves to enjoy—
Not likely, when all the young Lorens deploy.
They'll be there to-morrow, or even to-night.
100 They won't be too friendly—they may be polite—
To people they look on as having no right
To pick where they're picking. But we won't complain.
You ought to have seen how it looked in the rain,
The fruit mixed with water in layers of leaves,
105 Like two kinds of jewels, a vision for thieves."

A Servant to Servants[17]

I didn't make you know how glad I was
To have you come and camp here on our land.
I promised myself to get down some day
And see the way you lived, but I don't know!
5   With a houseful of hungry men to feed
I guess you'd find. . . . It seems to me
I can't express my feelings any more
Than I can raise my voice or want to lift
My hand (oh, I can lift it when I have to).
10   Did ever you feel so? I hope you never.
It's got so I don't even know for sure
Whether I *am* glad, sorry, or anything.
There's nothing but a voice-like left inside
That seems to tell me how I ought to feel,
15   And would feel if I wasn't all gone wrong.
You take the lake. I look and look at it.
I see it's a fair, pretty sheet of water.
I stand and make myself repeat out loud
The advantages it has, so long and narrow,
20   Like a deep piece of some old running river
Cut short off at both ends. It lies five miles
Straight away through the mountain notch
From the sink window where I wash the plates,
And all our storms come up toward the house,
25   Drawing the slow waves whiter and whiter and whiter.
It took my mind off doughnuts and soda biscuit
To step outdoors and take the water dazzle
A sunny morning, or take the rising wind
About my face and body and through my wrapper,
30   When a storm threatened from the Dragon's Den,
And a cold chill shivered across the lake.
I see it's a fair, pretty sheet of water,

Our Willoughby! How did you hear of it?
I expect, though, everyone's heard of it.
35   In a book about ferns? Listen to that!
You let things more like feathers regulate
Your going and coming. And you like it here?
I can see how you might. But I don't know!
It would be different if more people came,
40   For then there would be business. As it is,
The cottages Len built, sometimes we rent them,
Sometimes we don't. We've a good piece of shore
That ought to be worth something, and may yet.
But I don't count on it as much as Len.
45   He looks on the bright side of everything,
Including me. He thinks I'll be all right
With doctoring. But it's not medicine—
Lowe is the only doctor's dared to say so—
It's rest I want—there, I have said it out—
50   From cooking meals for hungry hired men
And washing dishes after them—from doing
Things over and over that just won't stay done.
By good rights I ought not to have so much
Put on me, but there seems no other way.
55   Len says one steady pull more ought to do it.
He says the best way out is always through.
And I agree to that, or in so far
As that I can see no way out but through—
Leastways for me—and then they'll be convinced.
60   It's not that Len don't want the best for me.
It was his plan our moving over in
Beside the lake from where that day I showed you
We used to live—ten miles from anywhere.
We didn't change without some sacrifice,

65 But Len went at it to make up the loss.
His work's a man's, of course, from sun to sun,
But he works when he works as hard as I do—
Though there's small profit in comparisons.
(Women and men will make them all the same.)
70 But work ain't all. Len undertakes too much.
He's into everything in town. This year
It's highways, and he's got too many men
Around him to look after that make waste.
They take advantage of him shamefully,
75 And proud, too, of themselves for doing so.
We have four here to board, great good-for-nothings,
Sprawling about the kitchen with their talk
While I fry their bacon. Much they care!
No more put out in what they do or say
80 Than if I wasn't in the room at all.
Coming and going all the time, they are:
I don't learn what their names are, let alone
Their characters, or whether they are safe
To have inside the house with doors unlocked.
85 I'm not afraid of them, though, if they're not
Afraid of me. There's two can play at that.
I have my fancies: it runs in the family.
My father's brother wasn't right. They kept him
Locked up for years back there at the old farm.
90 I've been away once—yes, I've been away.
The State Asylum. I was prejudiced;
I wouldn't have sent anyone of mine there;
You know the old idea—the only asylum
Was the poorhouse, and those who could afford,
95 Rather than send their folks to such a place,
Kept them at home; and it does seem more human.

But it's not so: the place is the asylum.
There they have every means proper to do with,
And you aren't darkening other people's lives—
Worse than no good to them, and they no good
To you in your condition; you can't know
Affection or the want of it in that state.
I've heard too much of the old-fashioned way.
My father's brother, he went mad quite young.
Some thought he had been bitten by a dog,
Because his violence took on the form
Of carrying his pillow in his teeth;
But it's more likely he was crossed in love,
Or so the story goes. It was some girl.
Anyway all he talked about was love.
They soon saw he would do someone a mischief
If he wa'n't kept strict watch of, and it ended
In father's building him a sort of cage,
Or room within a room, of hickory poles,
Like stanchions in the barn, from floor to ceiling,—
A narrow passage all the way around.
Anything they put in for furniture
He'd tear to pieces, even a bed to lie on.
So they made the place comfortable with straw,
Like a beast's stall, to ease their consciences.
Of course they had to feed him without dishes.
They tried to keep him clothed, but he paraded
With his clothes on his arm—all of his clothes.
Cruel—it sounds. I 'spose they did the best
They knew. And just when he was at the height,
Father and mother married, and mother came,
A bride, to help take care of such a creature,
And accommodate her young life to his.

That was what marrying father meant to her.
130 She had to lie and hear love things made dreadful
By his shouts in the night. He'd shout and shout
Until the strength was shouted out of him,
And his voice died down slowly from exhaustion.
He'd pull his bars apart like bow and bow-string,
135 And let them go and make them twang until
His hands had worn them smooth as any ox-bow.
And then he'd crow as if he thought that child's play—
The only fun he had. I've heard them say, though,
They found a way to put a stop to it.
140 He was before my time—I never saw him;
But the pen stayed exactly as it was
There in the upper chamber in the ell,
A sort of catch-all full of attic clutter.
I often think of the smooth hickory bars.
145 It got so I would say—you know, half fooling—
"It's time I took my turn upstairs in jail"—
Just as you will till it becomes a habit.
No wonder I was glad to get away.
Mind you, I waited till Len said the word.
150 I didn't want the blame if things went wrong.
I was glad though, no end, when we moved out,
And I looked to be happy, and I was,
As I said, for a while—but I don't know!
Somehow the change wore out like a prescription.
155 And there's more to it than just window-views
And living by a lake. I'm past such help—
Unless Len took the notion, which he won't,
And I won't ask him—it's not sure enough.
I 'spose I've got to go the road I'm going:
160 Other folks have to, and why shouldn't I?

I almost think if I could do like you,
Drop everything and live out on the ground—
But it might be, come night, I shouldn't like it,
Or a long rain. I should soon get enough,
165 And be glad of a good roof overhead.
I've lain awake thinking of you, I'll warrant,
More than you have yourself, some of these nights.
The wonder was the tents weren't snatched away
From over you as you lay in your beds.
170 I haven't courage for a risk like that.
Bless you, of course you'rt keeping me from work,
But the thing of it is, I need to *be* kept.
There's work enough to do—there's always that;
But behind's behind. The worst that you can do
175 Is set me back a little more behind.
I shan't catch up in this world, anyway.
I'd *rather* you'd not go unless you must.

After Apple-Picking

My long two-pointed ladder's sticking through a tree
Toward heaven still,
And there's a barrel that I didn't fill
Beside it, and there may be two or three
5   Apples I didn't pick upon some bough.
But I am done with apple-picking now.
Essence of winter sleep is on the night,
The scent of apples: I am drowsing off.
I cannot rub the strangeness from my sight
10   I got from looking through a pane of glass
I skimmed this morning from the drinking trough
And held against the world of hoary grass.
It melted, and I let it fall and break.
But I was well
15   Upon my way to sleep before it fell,
And I could tell
What form my dreaming was about to take.
Magnified apples appear and disappear,
Stem end and blossom end,
20   And every fleck of russet showing clear.
My instep arch not only keeps the ache,
It keeps the pressure of a ladder-round.
I feel the ladder sway as the boughs bend.
And I keep hearing from the cellar bin
25   The rumbling sound
Of load on load of apples coming in.
For I have had too much
Of apple-picking: I am overtired
Of the great harvest I myself desired.
30   There were ten thousand thousand fruit to touch,
Cherish in hand, lift down, and not let fall.
For all

That struck the earth,
No matter if not bruised or spiked with stubble,
35 Went surely to the cider-apple heap
As of no worth.
One can see what will trouble
This sleep of mine, whatever sleep it is.
Were he not gone,
40 The woodchuck could say whether it's like his
Long sleep, as I describe its coming on,
Or just some human sleep.

THE CODE

There were three in the meadow by the brook
Gathering up windrows, piling cocks of hay,
With an eye always lifted toward the west
Where an irregular sun-bordered cloud
5   Darkly advanced with a perpetual dagger
Flickering across its bosom. Suddenly
One helper, thrusting pitchfork in the ground,
Marched himself off the field and home. One stayed.
The town-bred farmer failed to understand.

10   "What is there wrong?"

                              "Something you just now said."

"What did I say?"

                              "About our taking pains."

"To cock the hay?—because it's going to shower?
I said that more than half an hour ago.
I said it to myself as much as you."

15   "You didn't know. But James is one big fool.
He thought you meant to find fault with his work.
That's what the average farmer would have meant.
James would take time, of course, to chew it over
Before he acted: he's just got round to act."

20   "He is a fool if that's the way he takes me."

"Don't let it bother you. You've found out something.
The hand that knows his business won't be told

To do work better or faster—those two things.
I'm as particular as any one:
25 Most likely I'd have served you just the same.
But I know you don't understand our ways.
You were just talking what was in your mind,
What was in all our minds, and you weren't hinting.
Tell you a story of what happened once:
30 I was up here in Salem at a man's
Named Sanders with a gang of four or five
Doing the haying. No one liked the boss.
He was one of the kind sports call a spider,
All wiry arms and legs that spread out wavy
35 From a humped body nigh as big's a biscuit.
But work! that man could work, especially
If by so doing he could get more work
Out of his hired help. I'm not denying
He was hard on himself. I couldn't find
40 That he kept any hours—not for himself.
Daylight and lantern-light were one to him:
I've heard him pounding in the barn all night.
But what he liked was someone to encourage.
Them that he couldn't lead he'd get behind
45 And drive, the way you can, you know, in mowing—
Keep at their heels and threaten to mow their legs off.
I'd seen about enough of his bulling tricks
(We call that bulling). I'd been watching him.
So when he paired off with me in the hayfield
50 To load the load, thinks I, Look out for trouble.
I built the load and topped it off; old Sanders
Combed it down with a rake and says, 'O.K.'
Everything went well till we reached the barn
With a big catch to empty in a bay.

55　You understand that meant the easy job
　　For the man up on top of throwing *down*
　　The hay and rolling it off wholesale,
　　Where on a mow it would have been slow lifting.
　　You wouldn't think a fellow'd need much urging
60　Under these circumstances, would you now?
　　But the old fool seizes his fork in both hands,
　　And looking up bewhiskered out of the pit,
　　Shouts like an army captain, 'Let her come!'
　　Thinks I, D'ye mean it? 'What was that you said?'
65　I asked out loud, so's there'd be no mistake,
　　'Did you say, Let her come?' 'Yes, let her come.'
　　He said it over, but he said it softer.
　　Never you say a thing like that to a man,
　　Not if he values what he is. God, I'd as soon
70　Murdered him as left out his middle name.
　　I'd built the load and knew right where to find it.
　　Two or three forkfuls I picked lightly round for
　　Like meditating, and then I just dug in
　　And dumped the rackful on him in ten lots.
75　I looked over the side once in the dust
　　And caught sight of him treading-water-like,
　　Keeping his head above. 'Damn ye,' I says,
　　'That gets ye!' He squeaked like a squeezed rat.
　　That was the last I saw or heard of him.
80　I cleaned the rack and drove out to cool off.
　　As I sat mopping hayseed from my neck,
　　And sort of waiting to be asked about it,
　　One of the boys sings out, 'Where's the old man?'
　　'I left him in the barn under the hay.
85　If ye want him, ye can go and dig him out.'
　　They realized from the way I swobbed my neck

More than was needed something must be up.
They headed for the barn; I stayed where I was.
They told me afterward. First they forked hay,
90   A lot of it, out into the barn floor.
Nothing! They listened for him. Not a rustle.
I guess they thought I'd spiked him in the temple
Before I buried him, or I couldn't have managed.
They excavated more. 'Go keep his wife
95   Out of the barn.' Someone looked in a window,
And curse me if he wasn't in the kitchen
Slumped way down in a chair, with both his feet
Stuck in the oven, the hottest day that summer.
He looked so clean disgusted from behind
100   There was no one that dared to stir him up,
Or let him know that he was being looked at.
Apparently I hadn't buried him
(I may have knocked him down); but my just trying
To bury him had hurt his dignity.
105   He had gone to the house so's not to meet me.
He kept away from us all afternoon.
We tended to his hay. We saw him out
After a while picking peas in his garden:
He couldn't keep away from doing something."

110   "Weren't you relieved to find he wasn't dead?"

"No! and yet I don't know—it's hard to say.
I went about to kill him fair enough."

"You took an awkward way. Did he discharge you?"

"Discharge me? No! He knew I did just right."

A governor it was proclaimed this time,
When all who would come seeking in New Hampshire
Ancestral memories might come together.
And those of the name Stark gathered in Bow,[18]
5   A rock-strewn town where farming has fallen off,
And sprout-lands flourish where the axe has gone.
Someone had literally run to earth
In an old cellar hole in a by-road
The origin of all the family there.
10   Thence they were sprung, so numerous a tribe
That now not all the houses left in town
Made shift to shelter them without the help
Of here and there a tent in grove and orchard.
They were at Bow, but that was not enough:
15   Nothing would do but they must fix a day
To stand together on the crater's verge
That turned them on the world, and try to fathom
The past and get some strangeness out of it.
But rain spoiled all. The day began uncertain,
20   With clouds low trailing and moments of rain that misted.
The young folk held some hope out to each other
Till well toward noon when the storm settled down
With a swish in the grass. "What if the others
Are there," they said. "It isn't going to rain."
25   Only one from a farm not far away
Strolled thither, not expecting he would find
Anyone else, but out of idleness.
One, and one other, yes, for there were two.
The second round the curving hillside road
30   Was a girl; and she halted some way off
To reconnoitre, and then made up her mind
At least to pass by and see who he was,

And perhaps to hear some word about the weather.
This was some Stark she didn't know. He nodded.
35 "No fête to-day," he said.

                              "It looks that way."
She swept the heavens, turning on her heel.
"I only idled down."

                  "I idled down."

Provision there had been for just such meeting
Of stranger cousins, in a family tree
40 Drawn on a sort of passport with the branch
Of the one bearing it done in detail—
Some zealous one's laborious device.
She made a sudden movement toward her bodice,
As one who clasps her heart. They laughed together.
45 "Stark?" he inquired. "No matter for the proof."

"Yes, Stark. And you?"

                        "I'm Stark." He drew his passport.

"You know we might not be and still be cousins:
The town is full of Chases, Lowes, and Baileys,
All claiming some priority in Starkness.
50 My mother was a Lane, yet might have married
Anyone upon earth and still her children
Would have been Starks, and doubtless here to-day."

"You riddle with your genealogy
Like a Viola.[19] I don't follow you."

55   "I only mean my mother was a Stark
    Several times over, and by marrying father
    No more than brought us back into the name."

    "One ought not to be thrown into confusion
    By a plain statement of relationship,
60   But I own what you say makes my head spin.
    You take my card—you seem so good at such things—
    And see if you can reckon our cousinship.
    Why not take seats here on the cellar wall
    And dangle feet among the raspberry vines?"

65   "Under the shelter of the family tree."

    "Just so—that ought to be enough protection."

    "Not from the rain. I think it's going to rain."

    "It's raining."

           "No, it's misting; let's be fair.
    Does the rain seem to you to cool the eyes?"

70   The situation was like this: the road,
    Bowed outward on the mountain half-way up,
    And disappeared and ended not far off.
    No one went home that way. The only house
    Beyond where they were was a shattered seedpod.
75   And below roared a brook hidden in trees,
    The sound of which was silence for the place.
    This he sat listening to till she gave judgment.

"On father's side, it seems, we're—let me see——"

"Don't be too technical.—You have three cards."

80 "Four cards, one yours, three mine, one for each branch
Of the Stark family I'm a member of."

"D'you know a person so related to herself
Is supposed to be mad."

            "I may be mad."

"You look so, sitting out here in the rain
85 Studying genealogy with me
You never saw before. What will we come to
With all this pride of ancestry, we Yankees?
I think we're all mad. Tell me why we're here
Drawn into town about this cellar hole
90 Like wild geese on a lake before a storm?
What do we see in such a hole, I wonder."

"The Indians had a myth of Chicamoztoc,[20]
Which means The Seven Caves that We Came out of.
This is the pit from which we Starks were digged."

95 "You must be learned. That's what you see in it?"

"And what do you see?"

            "Yes, what *do* I see?
First let me look. I see raspberry vines——"

"Oh, if you're going to use your eyes, just hear
What *I* see. It's a little, little boy,
As pale and dim as a match flame in the sun;
He's groping in the cellar after jam,
He thinks it's dark and it's flooded with daylight."

"He's nothing. Listen. When I lean like this
I can make out old Grandsir Stark distinctly,—
With his pipe in his mouth and his brown jug—
Bless you, it isn't Grandsir Stark, it's Granny,
But the pipe's there and smoking and the jug.
She's after cider, the old girl, she's thirsty;
Here's hoping she gets her drink and gets out safely."

"Tell me about her. Does she look like me?"

"She should, shouldn't she, you're so many times
Over descended from her. I believe
She does look like you. Stay the way you are.
The nose is just the same, and so's the chin—
Making allowance, making due allowance."

"You poor, dear, great, great, great, great Granny!"

"See that you get her greatness right. Don't stint her."

"Yes, it's important, though you think it isn't.
I won't be teased. But see how wet I am."

"Yes, you must go; we can't stay here for ever.
But wait until I give you a hand up.
A bead of silver water more or less

Strung on your hair won't hurt your summer looks.
I wanted to try something with the noise
125 That the brook raises in the empty valley.
We have seen visions—now consult the voices.
Something I must have learned riding in trains
When I was young. I used the roar
To set the voices speaking out of it,
130 Speaking or singing, and the band-music playing.
Perhaps you have the art of what I mean.
I've never listened in among the sounds
That a brook makes in such a wild descent.
It ought to give a purer oracle."

135 "It's as you throw a picture on a screen:
The meaning of it all is out of you;
The voices give you what you wish to hear."

"Strangely, it's anything they wish to give."

"Then I don't know. It must be strange enough.
140 I wonder if it's not your make-believe.
What do you think you're like to hear to-day?"

"From the sense of our having been together—
But why take time for what I'm like to hear?
I'll tell you what the voices really say.
145 You will do very well right where you are
A little longer. I mustn't feel too hurried,
Or I can't give myself to hear the voices."

"Is this some trance you are withdrawing into?"

"You must be very still; you mustn't talk."

150 "I'll hardly breathe."

                    "The voices seem to say——"

"I'm waiting."

              "Don't! The voices seem to say:
Call her Nausicaa, the unafraid
Of an acquaintance made adventurously."

"I let you say that—on consideration."

155 "I don't see very well how you can help it.
You want the truth. I speak but by the voices.
You see they know I haven't had your name,
Though what a name should matter between us——"

"I shall suspect——"

                    "Be good. The voices say:
160 Call her Nausicaa,[21] and take a timber
That you shall find lies in the cellar charred
Among the raspberries, and hew and shape it
For a door-sill or other corner piece
In a new cottage on the ancient spot.
165 The life is not yet all gone out of it.
And come and make your summer dwelling here,
And perhaps she will come, still unafraid,
And sit before you in the open door

With flowers in her lap until they fade,
170 But not come in across the sacred sill――"

"I wonder where your oracle is tending.
You can see that there's something wrong with it,
Or it would speak in dialect. Whose voice
Does it purport to speak in? Not old Grandsir's
175 Nor Granny's, surely. Call up one of them.
They have best right to be heard in this place."

"You seem so partial to our great-grandmother
(Nine times removed. Correct me if I err.)
You will be likely to regard as sacred
180 Anything she may say. But let me warn you,
Folks in her day were given to plain speaking.
You think you'd best tempt her at such a time?"

"It rests with us always to cut her off."

"Well then, it's Granny speaking: 'I dunnow!
185 Mebbe I'm wrong to take it as I do.
There ain't no names quite like the old ones though,
Nor never will be to my way of thinking.
One mustn't bear too hard on the new comers,
But there's a dite too many of them for comfort.
190 I should feel easier if I could see
More of the salt wherewith they're to be salted.
Son, you do as you're told! You take the timber――
It's as sound as the day when it was cut――
And begin over――' There, she'd better stop.
195 You can see what is troubling Granny, though.

But don't you think we sometimes make too much
Of the old stock? What counts is the ideals,
And those will bear some keeping still about."

"I can see we are going to be good friends."

200 "I like your 'going to be.' You said just now
It's going to rain."

                      "I know, and it was raining.
I let you say all that. But I must go now."

"You let me say it? on consideration?
How shall we say good-bye in such a case?"

205 "How shall we?"

                      "Will you leave the way to me?"

"No, I don't trust your eyes. You've said enough.
Now give me your hand up.—Pick me that flower."

"Where shall we meet again?"

                              "Nowhere but here
Once more before we meet elsewhere."

                                      "In rain?"

210 "It ought to be in rain. Sometime in rain.
In rain to-morrow, shall we, if it rains?
But if we must, in sunshine." So she went.

THE HOUSEKEEPER

I let myself in at the kitchen door.

"It's you," *she said.* "I can't get up. Forgive me
Not answering your knock. I can no more
Let people in than I can keep them out.
5   I'm getting too old for my size, I tell them.
My fingers are about all I've the use of
So's to take any comfort. I can sew:
I help out with this beadwork what I can."

"That's a smart pair of pumps you're beading there.
10 Who are they for?"

                              "You mean?—oh, for some miss.
I can't keep track of other people's daughters.
Lord, if I were to dream of everyone
Whose shoes I primped to dance in!"

                                      "And where's John?"

"Haven't you seen him? Strange what set you off
15 To come to his house when he's gone to yours.
You can't have passed each other. I know what:
He must have changed his mind and gone to Garlands.
He won't be long in that case. You can wait.
Though what good you can be, or anyone—
20 It's gone so far. You've heard? Estelle's run off."

"Yes, what's it all about? When did she go?"

"Two weeks since."

                "She's in earnest, it appears."

"I'm sure she won't come back. She's hiding somewhere.
I don't know where myself. John thinks I do.
25 He thinks I only have to say the word,
And she'll come back. But, bless you, I'm her mother—
I can't talk to her, and, Lord, if I could!"

"It will go hard with John. What will he do?
He can't find anyone to take her place."

30 "Oh, if you ask me that, what *will* he do?
He gets some sort of bakeshop meals together,
With me to sit and tell him everything,
What's wanted and how much and where it is.
But when I'm gone—of course I can't stay here:
35 Estelle's to take me when she's settled down.
He and I only hinder one another.
I tell them they can't get me through the door, though:
I've been built in here like a big church organ.
We've been here fifteen years."

                    "That's a long time
40 To live together and then pull apart.
How do you see him living when you're gone?
Two of you out will leave an empty house."

"I don't just see him living many years,
Left here with nothing but the furniture.

45 I hate to think of the old place when we're gone,
With the brook going by below the yard,
And no one here but hens blowing about.
If he could sell the place, but then, he can't:
No one will ever live on it again.
50 It's too run down. This is the last of it.
What I think he will do, is let things smash.
He'll sort of swear the time away. He's awful!
I never saw a man let family troubles
Make so much difference in his man's affairs.
55 He's just dropped everything. He's like a child.
I blame his being brought up by his mother.
He's got hay down that's been rained on three times.
He hoed a little yesterday for me:
I thought the growing things would do him good.
60 Something went wrong. I saw him throw the hoe
Sky-high with both hands. I can see it now—
Come here—I'll show you—in that apple tree.
That's no way for a man to do at his age:
He's fifty-five, you know, if he's a day."

65 "Aren't you afraid of him? What's that gun for?"

"Oh, that's been there for hawks since chicken-time.
John Hall touch me! Not if he knows his friends.
I'll say that for him, John's no threatener
Like some men folk. No one's afraid of him;
70 All is, he's made up his mind not to stand
What he has got to stand."

                              "Where is Estelle?

Couldn't one talk to her? What does she say?
You say you don't know where she is."

                          "Nor want to!
She thinks if it was bad to live with him,
75   It must be right to leave him."

                    "Which is wrong!"

"Yes, but he should have married her."

                          "I know."

"The strain's been too much for her all these years:
I can't explain it any other way.
It's different with a man, at least with John:
80   He knows he's kinder than the run of men.
Better than married ought to be as good
As married—that's what he has always said.
I know the way he's felt—but all the same!"

"I wonder why he doesn't marry her
85   And end it."

             "Too late now: she wouldn't have him.
He's given her time to think of something else.
That's his mistake. The dear knows my interest
Has been to keep the thing from breaking up.
This is a good home: I don't ask for better.
90   But when I've said, 'Why shouldn't they be married,'
He'd say, 'Why should they?' no more words than that."

"And after all why should they? John's been fair
I take it. What was his was always hers.
There was no quarrel about property."

95 "Reason enough, there was no property.
A friend or two as good as own the farm,
Such as it is. It isn't worth the mortgage."

"I mean Estelle has always held the purse."

"The rights of that are harder to get at.
100 I guess Estelle and I have filled the purse.
'Twas we let him have money, not he us.
John's a bad farmer. I'm not blaming him.
Take it year in, year out, he doesn't make much.
We came here for a home for me, you know,
105 Estelle to do the housework for the board
Of both of us. But look how it turns out:
She seems to have the housework, and besides
Half of the outdoor work, though as for that,
He'd say she does it more because she likes it.
110 You see our pretty things are all outdoors.
Our hens and cows and pigs are always better
Than folks like us have any business with.
Farmers around twice as well off as we
Haven't as good. They don't go with the farm.
115 One thing you can't help liking about John,
He's fond of nice things—too fond, some would say.
But Estelle don't complain: she's like him there.
She wants our hens to be the best there are.
You never saw this room before a show,
120 Full of lank, shivery, half-drowned birds

In separate coops, having their plumage done.
The smell of the wet feathers in the heat!
You spoke of John's not being safe to stay with.
You don't know what a gentle lot we are:
125   We wouldn't hurt a hen! You ought to see us
Moving a flock of hens from place to place.
We're not allowed to take them upside down,
All we can hold together by the legs.
Two at a time's the rule, one on each arm,
130   No matter how far and how many times
We have to go."

            "You mean that's John's idea."

"And we live up to it; or I don't know
What childishness he wouldn't give way to.
He manages to keep the upper hand
135   On his own farm. He's boss. But as to hens:
We fence our flowers in and the hens range.
Nothing's too good for them. We say it pays.
John likes to tell the offers he has had,
Twenty for this cock, twenty-five for that.
140   He never takes the money. If they're worth
  That much to sell, they're worth as much to keep.
Bless you, it's all expense, though. Reach me down
The little tin box on the cupboard shelf,
The upper shelf, the tin box. That's the one.
145   I'll show you. Here you are."

                    "What's this?"

                            "A bill—

For fifty dollars for one Langshang[22] cock—
Receipted. And the cock is in the yard."

"Not in a glass case, then?"

                              "He'd need a tall one:
He can eat off a barrel from the ground.
150 He's been in a glass case, as you may say,
The Crystal Palace, London.[23] He's imported.
John bought him, and we paid the bill with beads—
Wampum, I call it. Mind, we don't complain.
But you see, don't you, we take care of him."

155 "And like it, too. It makes it all the worse."

"It seems as if. And that's not all: he's helpless
In ways that I can hardly tell you of.
Sometimes he gets possessed to keep accounts
To see where all the money goes so fast.
160 You know how men will be ridiculous.
But it's just fun the way he gets bedeviled—
If he's untidy now, what will he be———?"

"It makes it all the worse. You must be blind."

"Estelle's the one. You needn't talk to me."

165 "Can't you and I get to the root of it?
What's the real trouble? What will satisfy her?"

"It's as I say: she's turned from him, that's all."

"But why, when she's well off? Is it the neighbours,
Being cut off from friends?"

                              "We have our friends.
170 That isn't it. Folks aren't afraid of us."

"She's let it worry her. You stood the strain,
And you're her mother."

                        "But I didn't always.
I didn't relish it along at first.
But I got wonted to it. And besides—
175 John said I was too old to have grandchildren.
But what's the use of talking when it's done?
She won't come back—it's worse than that—she can't."

"Why do you speak like that? What do you know?
What do you mean?—she's done harm to herself?"

180 "I mean she's married—married someone else."

"Oho, oho!"

                  "You don't believe me."

                              "Yes, I do,
Only too well. I knew there must be something!
So that was what was back. She's bad, that's all!"

"Bad to get married when she had the chance?"

185   "Nonsense! See what's she done! But who, who———"

"Who'd marry her straight out of such a mess?
Say it right out—no matter for her mother.
The man was found. I'd better name no names.
John himself won't imagine who he is."

190   "Then it's all up. I think I'll get away.
You'll be expecting John. I pity Estelle;
I suppose she deserves some pity, too.
You ought to have the kitchen to yourself
To break it to him. You may have the job."

195   "You needn't think you're going to get away.
John's almost here. I've had my eye on someone
Coming down Ryan's Hill. I thought 'twas him.
Here he is now. This box! Put it away.
And this bill."

            "What's the hurry? He'll unhitch."

200   "No, he won't, either. He'll just drop the reins
And turn Doll out to pasture, rig and all.
She won't get far before the wheels hang up
On something—there's no harm. See, there he is!
My, but he looks as if he must have heard!"

205   *John threw the door wide but he didn't enter.*
"How are you, neighbour? Just the man I'm after.
Isn't it Hell," *he said*. "I want to know.
Come out here if you want to hear me talk.

I'll talk to you, old woman, afterward.
210 I've got some news that maybe isn't news.
What are they trying to do to me, these two?"

"Do go along with him and stop his shouting."
She raised her voice against the closing door:
"Who wants to hear your news, you—dreadful fool?"

THE FEAR

A lantern light from deeper in the barn
Shone on a man and woman in the door
And threw their lurching shadows on a house
Near by, all dark in every glossy window.
5   A horse's hoof pawed once the hollow floor,
And the back of the gig they stood beside
Moved in a little. The man grasped a wheel,
The woman spoke out sharply, "Whoa, stand still!"
"I saw it just as plain as a white plate,"
10 She said, "as the light on the dashboard ran
Along the bushes at the roadside—a man's face.
You *must* have seen it too."

                "I didn't see it.
Are you sure——"

           "Yes, I'm sure!"

                  "—it was a face?"

"Joel, I'll have to look. I can't go in,
15 I can't, and leave a thing like that unsettled.
Doors locked and curtains drawn will make no difference.
I always have felt strange when we came home
To the dark house after so long an absence,
And the key rattled loudly into place
20 Seemed to warn someone to be getting out
At one door as we entered at another.
What if I'm right, and someone all the time—
Don't hold my arm!"

           "I say it's someone passing."

"You speak as if this were a travelled road.
You forget where we are. What is beyond
That he'd be going to or coming from
At such an hour of night, and on foot too.
What was he standing still for in the bushes?"

"It's not so very late—it's only dark.
There's more in it than you're inclined to say.
Did he look like——?"

                 "He looked like anyone.
I'll never rest to-night unless I know.
Give me the lantern."

                    "You don't want the lantern."

She pushed past him and got it for herself.

"You're not to come," she said. "This is my business.
If the time's come to face it, I'm the one
To put it the right way. He'd never dare—
Listen! He kicked a stone. Hear that, hear that!
He's coming towards us. Joel, *go* in—please.
Hark!—I don't hear him now. But please go in."

"In the first place you can't make me believe it's——"

"It is—or someone else he's sent to watch.
And now's the time to have it out with him
While we know definitely where he is.
Let him get off and he'll be everywhere
Around us, looking out of trees and bushes

Till I shan't dare to set a foot outdoors.
And I can't stand it. Joel, let me go!"

"But it's nonsense to think he'd care enough."

50   "You mean you couldn't understand his caring.
Oh, but you see he hadn't had enough—
Joel, I won't—I won't—I promise you.
We mustn't say hard things. You mustn't either."

"I'll be the one, if anybody goes!
55   But you give him the advantage with this light.
What couldn't he do to us standing here!
And if to see was what he wanted, why
He has seen all there was to see and gone."

He appeared to forget to keep his hold,
60   But advanced with her as she crossed the grass.

"What do you want?" she cried to all the dark.
She stretched up tall to overlook the light
That hung in both hands hot against her skirt.

"There's no one; so you're wrong," he said.

                                          "There is.—
65   What do you want?" she cried, and then herself
Was startled when an answer really came.

"Nothing." It came from well along the road.

She reached a hand to Joel for support:
The smell of scorching woollen made her faint.

70 "What are you doing round this house at night?"

"Nothing." A pause: there seemed no more to say.

And then the voice again: "You seem afraid.
I saw by the way you whipped up the horse.
I'll just come forward in the lantern light
And let you see."

75   "Yes, do.—Joel, go back!"

She stood her ground against the noisy steps
That came on, but her body rocked a little.

"You see," the voice said.

                        "Oh." She looked and looked.

"You don't see—I've a child here by the hand."

80 "What's a child doing at this time of night——?"

"Out walking. Every child should have the memory
Of at least one long-after-bedtime walk.
What, son?"

                "Then I should think you'd try to find
Somewhere to walk——"

                        "The highway as it happens—
85 We're stopping for the fortnight down at Dean's."

"But if that's all—Joel—you realize—
You won't think anything. You understand?
You understand that we have to be careful.
This is a very, very lonely place.
90 Joel!" She spoke as if she couldn't turn.
The swinging lantern lengthened to the ground,
It touched, it struck it, clattered and went out.

THE SELF-SEEKER

"Willis, I didn't want you here to-day:
The lawyer's coming for the company.
I'm going to sell my soul, or, rather, feet.
Five hundred dollars for the pair, you know."

5   "With you the feet have nearly been the soul;
And if you're going to sell them to the devil,
I want to see you do it. When's he coming?"

"I half suspect you knew, and came on purpose
To try to help me drive a better bargain."

10 "Well, if it's true! Yours are no common feet.
The lawyer don't know what it is he's buying:
So many miles you might have walked you won't walk.
You haven't run your forty orchids down.
What does he think?—How *are* the blessed feet?[24]
15 The doctor's sure you're going to walk again?"

"He thinks I'll hobble. It's both legs and feet."

"They must be terrible—I mean to look at."

"I haven't dared to look at them uncovered.
Through the bed blankets I remind myself
20 Of a starfish laid out with rigid points."

"The wonder is it hadn't been your head."

"It's hard to tell you how I managed it.
When I saw the shaft had me by the coat,

I didn't try too long to pull away,
25 Or fumble for my knife to cut away,
I just embraced the shaft and rode it out—
Till Weiss shut off the water in the wheel-pit.
That's how I think I didn't lose my head.
But my legs got their knocks against the ceiling."

30 "Awful. Why didn't they throw off the belt
Instead of going clear down in the wheel-pit?"

"They say some time was wasted on the belt—
Old streak of leather—doesn't love me much
Because I make him spit fire at my knuckles,
35 The way Ben Franklin used to make the kite-string.
That must be it. Some days he won't stay on.
That day a woman couldn't coax him off.
He's on his rounds now with his tail in his mouth
Snatched right and left across the silver pulleys.
40 Everything goes the same without me there.
You can hear the small buzz saws whine, the big saw
Caterwaul to the hills around the village
As they both bite the wood. It's all our music.
One ought as a good villager to like it.
45 No doubt it has a sort of prosperous sound,
And it's our life."

                    "Yes, when it's not our death."

"You make that sound as if it wasn't so
With everything. What we live by we die by.
I wonder where my lawyer is. His train's in.
50 I want this over with; I'm hot and tired."

"You're getting ready to do something foolish."

"Watch for him, will you, Will? You let him in.
I'd rather Mrs. Corbin didn't know;
I've boarded here so long, she thinks she owns me.
55 You're bad enough to manage without her."

"And I'm going to be worse instead of better.
You've got to tell me how far this is gone;
Have you agreed to any price?"

                              "Five hundred.
Five hundred—five—five! One, two, three, four, five.
60 You needn't look at me."

                      "I don't believe you."

"I told you, Willis, when you first came in.
Don't you be hard on me. I have to take
What I can get. You see they have the feet,
Which gives them the advantage in the trade.
65 I can't get back the feet in any case."

"But your flowers, man, you're selling out your flowers."

"Yes, that's one way to put it—all the flowers
Of every kind everywhere in this region
For the next forty summers—call it forty.
70 But I'm not selling those, I'm giving them,
They never earned me so much as one cent:

Money can't pay me for the loss of them.
No, the five hundred was the sum they named
To pay the doctor's bill and tide me over.
75 It's that or fight, and I don't want to fight—
I just want to get settled in my life,
Such as it's going to be, and know the worst,
Or best—it may not be so bad. The firm
Promise me all the shooks I want to nail."

80 "But what about your flora of the valley?"

"You have me there. But that—you didn't think
That was worth money to me? Still I own
It goes against me not to finish it
For the friends it might bring me. By the way,
85 I had a letter from Burroughs—did I tell you?—
About my *Cyprepedium reginæ*;[25]
He says it's not reported so far north.
There! there's the bell. He's rung. But you go down
And bring him up, and don't let Mrs. Corbin.—
90 Oh, well, we'll soon be through with it. I'm tired."

Willis brought up besides the Boston lawyer
A little barefoot girl who in the noise
Of heavy footsteps in the old frame house,
And baritone importance of the lawyer,
95 Stood for a while unnoticed with her hands
Shyly behind her.

              "Well, and how is Mister ———"

The lawyer was already in his satchel
As if for papers that might bear the name
He hadn't at command. "You must excuse me,
I dropped in at the mill and was detained."

"Looking round, I suppose," said Willis.

                                        "Yes,
Well, yes."

            "Hear anything that might prove useful?"

The Broken One saw Anne. "Why, here is Anne.
What do you want, dear? Come, stand by the bed;
Tell me what is it?" Anne just wagged her dress
With both hands held behind her. "Guess," she said.
"Oh, guess which hand? My, my! Once on a time
I knew a lovely way to tell for certain
By looking in the ears. But I forget it.
Er, let me see. I think I'll take the right.
That's sure to be right even if it's wrong.
Come, hold it out. Don't change.—A Ram's Horn orchid!
A Ram's Horn! What would I have got, I wonder,
If I had chosen left. Hold out the left.
Another Ram's Horn! Where did you find those,
Under what beech tree, on what woodchuck's knoll?"
Anne looked at the large lawyer at her side,
And thought she wouldn't venture on so much.

"Were there no others?"

                        "There were four or five.
I knew you wouldn't let me pick them all."

"I wouldn't—so I wouldn't. You're the girl!
You see Anne has her lesson learned by heart."

"I wanted there should be some there next year."

"Of course you did. You left the rest for seed,
125   And for the backwoods woodchuck. You're the girl!
A Ram's Horn orchid seedpod for a woodchuck
Sounds something like. Better than farmer's beans
To a discriminating appetite,
Though the Ram's Horn is seldom to be had
130   In bushel lots—doesn't come on the market.
But, Anne, I'm troubled; have you told me all?
You're hiding something. That's as bad as lying.
You ask this lawyer man. And it's not safe
With a lawyer at hand to find you out.
135   Nothing is hidden from some people, Anne.
You don't tell me that where you found a Ram's Horn
You didn't find a Yellow Lady's Slipper.
What did I tell you? What? I'd blush, I would.
Don't you defend yourself. If it was there,
140   Where is it now, the Yellow Lady's Slipper?"

"Well, wait—it's common—it's too *common*."

                                              "Common?
The Purple Lady's Slipper's commoner."

"I didn't bring a Purple Lady's Slipper
To *You*—to you I mean—they're both too common."

145   The lawyer gave a laugh among his papers
As if with some idea that she had scored.

- 127 -

"I've broken Anne of gathering bouquets.
It's not fair to the child. It can't be helped though:
Pressed into service means pressed out of shape.
150 Somehow I'll make it right with her—she'll see.
She's going to do my scouting in the field,
Over stone walls and all along a wood
And by a river bank for water flowers,
The floating Heart, with small leaf like a heart,
155 And at the *sinus* under water a fist
Of little fingers all kept down but one,
And that thrust up to blossom in the sun
As if to say, "You! You're the Heart's desire."
Anne has a way with flowers to take the place
160 Of that she's lost: she goes down on one knee
And lifts their faces by the chin to hers
And says their names, and leaves them where they are."

The lawyer wore a watch the case of which
Was cunningly devised to make a noise
165 Like a small pistol when he snapped it shut
At such a time as this. He snapped it now.

"Well, Anne, go, dearie. Our affair will wait.
The lawyer man is thinking of his train.
He wants to give me lots and lots of money
170 Before he goes, because I hurt myself,
And it may take him I don't know how long.
But put our flowers in water first. Will, help her:
The pitcher's too full for her. There's no cup?
Just hook them on the inside of the pitcher.
175 Now run.—Get out your documents! You see
I have to keep on the good side of Anne.

I'm a great boy to think of number one.
And you can't blame me in the place I'm in.
Who will take care of my necessities
180 Unless I do?"

               "A pretty interlude,"
The lawyer said. "I'm sorry, but my train—
Luckily terms are all agreed upon.
You only have to sign your name. Right—there."

"You, Will, stop making faces. Come round here
185 Where you can't make them. What is it you want?
I'll put you out with Anne. Be good or go."

"You don't mean you will sign that thing unread?"

"Make yourself useful then, and read it for me.
Isn't it something I have seen before?"

190 "You'll find it is. Let your friend look at it."

"Yes, but all that takes time, and I'm as much
In haste to get it over with as you.
But read it, read it. That's right, draw the curtain:
Half the time I don't know what's troubling me.—
195 What do you say, Will? Don't you be a fool,
You! crumpling folkses legal documents.
Out with it if you've any real objection."

"Five hundred dollars!"

                  "What would you think right?"

"A thousand wouldn't be a cent too much;
200 You know it, Mr. Lawyer. The sin is
Accepting anything before he knows
Whether he's ever going to walk again.
It smells to me like a dishonest trick."

"I think—I think—from what I heard to-day—
205 And saw myself—he would be ill-advised——"

"What did you hear, for instance?" Willis said.

"Now the place where the accident occurred—"

The Broken One was twisted in his bed.
"This is between you two apparently.
210 Where I come in is what I want to know.
You stand up to it like a pair of cocks.
Go outdoors if you want to fight. Spare me.
When you come back, I'll have the papers signed.
Will pencil do? Then, please, your fountain pen.
215 One of you hold my head up from the pillow."

Willis flung off the bed. "I wash my hands—
I'm no match—no, and don't pretend to be——"

The lawyer gravely capped his fountain pen.
"You're doing the wise thing: you won't regret it.
220 We're very sorry for you."

                              Willis sneered:
"Who's *we?*—some stockholders in Boston?
I'll go outdoors, by gad, and won't come back."

"Willis, bring Anne back with you when you come.
Yes. Thanks for caring. Don't mind Will: he's savage.
225   He thinks you ought to pay me for my flowers.
You don't know what I mean about the flowers.
Don't stop to try to now. You'll miss your train.
Good-bye." He flung his arms around his face.

The Wood-Pile

Out walking in the frozen swamp one grey day
I paused and said, "I will turn back from here.
No, I will go on farther—and we shall see."
The hard snow held me, save where now and then
5   One foot went down. The view was all in lines
Straight up and down of tall slim trees
Too much alike to mark or name a place by
So as to say for certain I was here
Or somewhere else: I was just far from home.
10 A small bird flew before me. He was careful
To put a tree between us when he lighted,
And say no word to tell me who he was
Who was so foolish as to think what *he* thought.
He thought that I was after him for a feather—
15 The white one in his tail; like one who takes
Everything said as personal to himself.
One flight out sideways would have undeceived him.
And then there was a pile of wood for which
I forgot him and let his little fear
20 Carry him off the way I might have gone,
Without so much as wishing him good-night.
He went behind it to make his last stand.
It was a cord of maple, cut and split
And piled—and measured, four by four by eight.
25 And not another like it could I see.
No runner tracks in this year's snow looped near it.
And it was older sure than this year's cutting,
Or even last year's or the year's before.
The wood was grey and the bark warping off it
30 And the pile somewhat sunken. Clematis
Had wound strings round and round it like a bundle.
What held it though on one side was a tree

Still growing, and on one a stake and prop,
These latter about to fall. I thought that only
35 Someone who lived in turning to fresh tasks
Could so forget his handiwork on which
He spent himself, the labour of his axe,
And leave it there far from a useful fireplace
To warm the frozen swamp as best it could
40 With the slow smokeless burning of decay.

GOOD HOURS[26]

I had for my winter evening walk—
No one at all with whom to talk,
But I had the cottages in a row
Up to their shining eyes in snow.

5   And I thought I had the folk within:
I had the sound of a violin;
I had a glimpse through curtain laces
Of youthful forms and youthful faces.

I had such company outward bound.
10 I went till there were no cottages found.
I turned and repented, but coming back
I saw no window but that was black.

Over the snow my creaking feet
Disturbed the slumbering village street
15 Like profanation, by your leave,
At ten o'clock of a winter eve.

MOUNTAIN INTERVAL²⁷

TO YOU

WHO LEAST NEED REMINDING

that before this interval of the South Branch under black mountains, there was another interval, the Upper at Plymouth, where we walked in spring beyond the covered bridge; but that the first interval of all was the old farm, our brook interval, so called by the man we had it from in sale.

THE ROAD NOT TAKEN

Two roads diverged in a yellow wood,
And sorry I could not travel both
And be one traveler, long I stood
And looked down one as far as I could
5 To where it bent in the undergrowth;

Then took the other, as just as fair,
And having perhaps the better claim,
Because it was grassy and wanted wear;
Though as for that the passing there
10 Had worn them really about the same,

And both that morning equally lay
In leaves no step had trodden black.
Oh, I kept the first for another day!
Yet knowing how way leads on to way,
15 I doubted if I should ever come back.

I shall be telling this with a sigh
Somewhere ages and ages hence:
Two roads diverged in a wood, and I—
I took the one less traveled by,
20 And that has made all the difference.

CHRISTMAS TREES
(A Christmas Circular Letter)

The city had withdrawn into itself
And left at last the country to the country;
When between whirls of snow not come to lie
And whirls of foliage not yet laid, there drove
5   A stranger to our yard, who looked the city,
Yet did in country fashion in that there
He sat and waited till he drew us out
A-buttoning coats to ask him who he was.
He proved to be the city come again
10   To look for something it had left behind
And could not do without and keep its Christmas.
He asked if I would sell my Christmas trees;
My woods—the young fir balsams like a place
Where houses all are churches and have spires.
15   I hadn't thought of them as Christmas trees.
I doubt if I was tempted for a moment
To sell them off their feet to go in cars
And leave the slope behind the house all bare,
Where the sun shines now no warmer than the moon.
20   I'd hate to have them know it if I was.
Yet more I'd hate to hold my trees except
As others hold theirs or refuse for them,
Beyond the time of profitable growth,
The trial by market everything must come to.
25   I dallied so much with the thought of selling.
Then whether from mistaken courtesy
And fear of seeming short of speech, or whether
From hope of hearing good of what was mine,
I said, "There aren't enough to be worth while."

30 "I could soon tell how many they would cut,
    You let me look them over."

                              "You could look.
    But don't expect I'm going to let you have them."
    Pasture they spring in, some in clumps too close
    That lop each other of boughs, but not a few
35 Quite solitary and having equal boughs
    All round and round. The latter he nodded "Yes" to,
    Or paused to say beneath some lovelier one,
    With a buyer's moderation, "That would do."
    I thought so too, but wasn't there to say so.
40 We climbed the pasture on the south, crossed over,
    And came down on the north.

                              He said, "A thousand."

    "A thousand Christmas trees!—at what apiece?"

    He felt some need of softening that to me:
    "A thousand trees would come to thirty dollars."

45 Then I was certain I had never meant
    To let him have them. Never show surprise!
    But thirty dollars seemed so small beside
    The extent of pasture I should strip, three cents
    (For that was all they figured out apiece),
50 Three cents so small beside the dollar friends
    I should be writing to within the hour
    Would pay in cities for good trees like those,
    Regular vestry-trees whole Sunday Schools

Could hang enough on to pick off enough.
55 A thousand Christmas trees I didn't know I had!
Worth three cents more to give away than sell,
As may be shown by a simple calculation.
Too bad I couldn't lay one in a letter.
I can't help wishing I could send you one,
60 In wishing you herewith a Merry Christmas.

An Old Man's Winter Night

All out of doors looked darkly in at him
Through the thin frost, almost in separate stars,
That gathers on the pane in empty rooms.
What kept his eyes from giving back the gaze
5   Was the lamp tilted near them in his hand.
What kept him from remembering what it was
That brought him to that creaking room was age.
He stood with barrels round him—at a loss.
And having scared the cellar under him
10   In clomping there, he scared it once again
In clomping off;—and scared the outer night,
Which has its sounds, familiar, like the roar
Of trees and crack of branches, common things,
But nothing so like beating on a box.
15   A light he was to no one but himself
Where now he sat, concerned with he knew what,
A quiet light, and then not even that.
He consigned to the moon, such as she was,
So late-arising, to the broken moon
20   As better than the sun in any case
For such a charge, his snow upon the roof,
His icicles along the wall to keep;
And slept. The log that shifted with a jolt
Once in the stove, disturbed him and he shifted,
25   And eased his heavy breathing, but still slept.
One aged man—one man—can't fill a house,
A farm, a countryside, or if he can,
It's thus he does it of a winter night.

A Patch of Old Snow

There's a patch of old snow in a corner
    That I should have guessed
Was a blow-away paper the rain
    Had brought to rest.

5 It is speckled with grime as if
    Small print overspread it,
The news of a day I've forgotten—
    If I ever read it.

IN THE HOME STRETCH

She stood against the kitchen sink, and looked
Over the sink out through a dusty window
At weeds the water from the sink made tall.
She wore her cape; her hat was in her hand.
5   Behind her was confusion in the room,
Of chairs turned upside down to sit like people
In other chairs, and something, come to look,
For every room a house has—parlor, bed-room,
And dining-room—thrown pell-mell in the kitchen.
10 And now and then a smudged, infernal face
Looked in a door behind her and addressed
Her back. She always answered without turning.

"Where will I put this walnut bureau, lady?"
"Put it on top of something that's on top
15 Of something else," she laughed. "Oh, put it where
You can to-night, and go. It's almost dark;
You must be getting started back to town."
Another blackened face thrust in and looked
And smiled, and when she did not turn, spoke gently,
20 "What are you seeing out the window, *lady?*"

"Never was I beladied so before.
Would evidence of having been called lady
More than so many times make me a lady
In common law, I wonder."

                        "But I ask,
25 What are you seeing out the window, lady?"

"What I'll be seeing more of in the years
To come as here I stand and go the round
Of many plates with towels many times."

"And what is that? You only put me off."

30 "Rank weeds that love the water from the dish-pan
More than some women like the dish-pan, Joe;
A little stretch of mowing-field for you;
Not much of that until I come to woods
That end all. And it's scarce enough to call
A view."

35   "And yet you think you like it, dear?"

"That's what you're so concerned to know! You hope
I like it. Bang goes something big away
Off there upstairs. The very tread of men
As great as those is shattering to the frame
40 Of such a little house. Once left alone,
You and I, dear, will go with softer steps
Up and down stairs and through the rooms, and none
But sudden winds that snatch them from our hands
Will ever slam the doors."

                              "I think you see
45 More than you like to own to out that window."

"No; for besides the things I tell you of,
I only see the years. They come and go
In alternation with the weeds, the field,
The wood."

"What kind of years?"

"Why, latter years—
Different from early years."

"I see them, too.
You didn't count them?"

"No, the further off
So ran together that I didn't try to.
It can scarce be that they would be in number
We'd care to know, for we are not young now.
55 And bang goes something else away off there.
It sounds as if it were the men went down,
And every crash meant one less to return
To lighted city streets we, too, have known,
But now are giving up for country darkness."

60 "Come from that window where you see too much for me,
And take a livelier view of things from here.
They're going. Watch this husky swarming up
Over the wheel into the sky-high seat,
Lighting his pipe now, squinting down his nose
65 At the flame burning downward as he sucks it."

"See how it makes his nose-side bright, a proof
How dark it's getting. Can you tell what time
It is by that? Or by the moon? The new moon!
What shoulder did I see her over? Neither.
70 A wire she is of silver, as new as we
To everything. Her light won't last us long.
It's something, though, to know we're going to have her

- 145 -

Night after night and stronger every night
To see us through our first two weeks. But, Joe,
75 The stove! Before they go! Knock on the window;
Ask them to help you get it on its feet.
We stand here dreaming. Hurry! Call them back!"

"They're not gone yet."

                              "We've got to have the stove,
Whatever else we want for. And a light.
80 Have we a piece of candle if the lamp
And oil are buried out of reach?"

                              Again
The house was full of tramping, and the dark,
Door-filling men burst in and seized the stove.
A cannon-mouth-like hole was in the wall,
85 To which they set it true by eye; and then
Came up the jointed stovepipe in their hands,
So much too light and airy for their strength
It almost seemed to come ballooning up,
Slipping from clumsy clutches toward the ceiling.
90 "A fit!" said one, and banged a stovepipe shoulder.
"It's good luck when you move in to begin
With good luck with your stovepipe. Never mind,
It's not so bad in the country, settled down,
When people're getting on in life. You'll like it."
95 Joe said: "You big boys ought to find a farm,
And make good farmers, and leave other fellows
The city work to do. There's not enough
For everybody as it is in there."
"God!" one said wildly, and, when no one spoke:

100 "Say that to Jimmy here. He needs a farm."
But Jimmy only made his jaw recede
Fool-like, and rolled his eyes as if to say
He saw himself a farmer. Then there was a French boy
Who said with seriousness that made them laugh,
105 "Ma friend, you ain't know what it is you're ask."
He doffed his cap and held it with both hands
Across his chest to make as 'twere a bow:
"We're giving you our chances on de farm."
And then they all turned to with deafening boots
110 And put each other bodily out of the house.
"Goodby to them! We puzzle them. They think—
I don't know what they think we see in what
They leave us to: that pasture slope that seems
The back some farm presents us; and your woods
115 To northward from your window at the sink,
Waiting to steal a step on us whenever
We drop our eyes or turn to other things,
As in the game 'Ten-step' the children play."

"Good boys they seemed, and let them love the city.
120 All they could say was 'God!' when you proposed
Their coming out and making useful farmers."

"Did they make something lonesome go through you?
It would take more than them to sicken you—
Us of our bargain. But they left us so
125 As to our fate, like fools past reasoning with.
They almost shook *me*."

                    "It's all so much
What we have always wanted, I confess

It's seeming bad for a moment makes it seem
Even worse still, and so on down, down, down.
130 It's nothing; it's their leaving us at dusk.
I never bore it well when people went.
The first night after guests have gone, the house
Seems haunted or exposed. I always take
A personal interest in the locking up
135 At bedtime; but the strangeness soon wears off."
He fetched a dingy lantern from behind
A door. "There's that we didn't lose! And these!"—
Some matches he unpocketed. "For food—
The meals we've had no one can take from us.
140 I wish that everything on earth were just
As certain as the meals we've had. I wish
The meals we haven't had were, anyway.
What have you you know where to lay your hands on?"

"The bread we bought in passing at the store.
There's butter somewhere, too."

145   "Let's rend the bread.
I'll light the fire for company for you;
You'll not have any other company
Till Ed begins to get out on a Sunday
To look us over and give us his idea
150 Of what wants pruning, shingling, breaking up.
He'll know what he would do if he were we,
And all at once. He'll plan for us and plan
To help us, but he'll take it out in planning.
Well, you can set the table with the loaf.
155 Let's see you find your loaf. I'll light the fire.

I like chairs occupying other chairs
Not offering a lady—"

           "There again, Joe!
You're tired."

         "I'm drunk-nonsensical tired out;
Don't mind a word I say. It's a day's work
160 To empty one house of all household goods
And fill another with 'em fifteen miles away,
Although you do no more than dump them down."

"Dumped down in paradise we are and happy."

"It's all so much what I have always wanted,
165 I can't believe it's what you wanted, too."

"Shouldn't you like to know?"

              "I'd like to know
If it is what you wanted, then how much
You wanted it for me."

          "A troubled conscience!
You don't want me to tell if *I* don't know."

170 "I don't want to find out what can't be known.
But who first said the word to come?"

             "My dear,
It's who first thought the thought. You're searching, Joe,

For things that don't exist; I mean beginnings.
Ends and beginnings—there are no such things.
There are only middles."

                    "What is this?"

175   "This life?
Our sitting here by lantern–light together
Amid the wreckage of a former home?
You won't deny the lantern isn't new.
The stove is not, and you are not to me,
Nor I to you."

180   "Perhaps you never were?"

"It would take me forever to recite
All that's not new in where we find ourselves.
New is a word for fools in towns who think
Style upon style in dress and thought at last
185   Must get somewhere. I've heard you say as much.
No, this is no beginning."

                    "Then an end?"

"End is a gloomy word."

                    "Is it too late
To drag you out for just a good-night call
On the old peach trees on the knoll to grope
190   By starlight in the grass for a last peach
The neighbors may not have taken as their right

When the house wasn't lived in? I've been looking:
I doubt if they have left us many grapes.
Before we set ourselves to right the house,
195 The first thing in the morning, out we go
To go the round of apple, cherry, peach,
Pine, alder, pasture, mowing, well, and brook.
All of a farm it is."

               "I know this much:
I'm going to put you in your bed, if first
200 I have to make you build it. Come, the light."

When there was no more lantern in the kitchen,
The fire got out through crannies in the stove
And danced in yellow wrigglers on the ceiling,
As much at home as if they'd always danced there.

THE TELEPHONE

"When I was just as far as I could walk
From here to-day,
There was an hour
All still
5   When leaning with my head against a flower
I heard you talk.
Don't say I didn't, for I heard you say—
You spoke from that flower on the window sill—
Do you remember what it was you said?"

10 "First tell me what it was you thought you heard."

"Having found the flower and driven a bee away,
I leaned my head,
And holding by the stalk,
I listened and I thought I caught the word—
15 What was it? Did you call me by my name?
Or did you say—
Someone said 'Come'—I heard it as I bowed."

"I may have thought as much, but not aloud."

"Well, so I came."

MEETING AND PASSING

As I went down the hill along the wall
There was a gate I had leaned at for the view
And had just turned from when I first saw you
As you came up the hill. We met. But all
We did that day was mingle great and small
Footprints in summer dust as if we drew
The figure of our being less than two
But more than one as yet. Your parasol

Pointed the decimal off with one deep thrust.
And all the time we talked you seemed to see
Something down there to smile at in the dust.
(Oh, it was without prejudice to me!)
Afterward I went past what you had passed
Before we met and you what I had passed.

Hyla Brook

By June our brook's run out of song and speed.
Sought for much after that, it will be found
Either to have gone groping underground
(And taken with it all the Hyla breed[28]
5   That shouted in the mist a month ago,
Like ghost of sleigh-bells in a ghost of snow)—
Or flourished and come up in jewel-weed,
Weak foliage that is blown upon and bent
Even against the way its waters went.
10   Its bed is left a faded paper sheet
Of dead leaves stuck together by the heat—
A brook to none but who remember long.
This as it will be seen is other far
Than with brooks taken otherwhere in song.
15   We love the things we love for what they are.

THE OVEN BIRD[29]

There is a singer everyone has heard,
Loud, a mid-summer and a mid-wood bird,
Who makes the solid tree trunks sound again.
He says that leaves are old and that for flowers
5   Mid-summer is to spring as one to ten.
He says the early petal-fall is past
When pear and cherry bloom went down in showers
On sunny days a moment overcast;
And comes that other fall we name the fall.
10 He says the highway dust is over all.
The bird would cease and be as other birds
But that he knows in singing not to sing.
The question that he frames in all but words
Is what to make of a diminished thing.

BOND AND FREE

Love has earth to which she clings
With hills and circling arms about—
Wall within wall to shut fear out.
But Thought has need of no such things,
5   For Thought has a pair of dauntless wings.

On snow and sand and turf, I see
Where Love has left a printed trace
With straining in the world's embrace.
And such is Love and glad to be.
10   But Thought has shaken his ankles free.

Thought cleaves the interstellar gloom
And sits in Sirius' disc all night,
Till day makes him retrace his flight,
With smell of burning on every plume,
15   Back past the sun to an earthly room.

His gains in heaven are what they are.
Yet some say Love by being thrall
And simply staying possesses all
In several beauty that Thought fares far
20   To find fused in another star.

BIRCHES

When I see birches bend to left and right
Across the lines of straighter darker trees,
I like to think some boy's been swinging them.
But swinging doesn't bend them down to stay.
5   Ice-storms do that. Often you must have seen them
Loaded with ice a sunny winter morning
After a rain. They click upon themselves
As the breeze rises, and turn many-colored
As the stir cracks and crazes their enamel.
10 Soon the sun's warmth makes them shed crystal shells
Shattering and avalanching on the snow-crust—
Such heaps of broken glass to sweep away
You'd think the inner dome of heaven had fallen.[30]
They are dragged to the withered bracken by the load,
15 And they seem not to break; though once they are bowed
So low for long, they never right themselves:
You may see their trunks arching in the woods
Years afterwards, trailing their leaves on the ground
Like girls on hands and knees that throw their hair
20 Before them over their heads to dry in the sun.
But I was going to say when Truth broke in
With all her matter-of-fact about the ice-storm
(Now am I free to be poetical?)
I should prefer to have some boy bend them
25 As he went out and in to fetch the cows—
Some boy too far from town to learn baseball,
Whose only play was what he found himself,
Summer or winter, and could play alone.
One by one he subdued his father's trees
30 By riding them down over and over again
Until he took the stiffness out of them,
And not one but hung limp, not one was left

For him to conquer. He learned all there was
To learn about not launching out too soon
35 And so not carrying the tree away
Clear to the ground. He always kept his poise
To the top branches, climbing carefully
With the same pains you use to fill a cup
Up to the brim, and even above the brim.
40 Then he flung outward, feet first, with a swish,
Kicking his way down through the air to the ground.
So was I once myself a swinger of birches.
And so I dream of going back to be.
It's when I'm weary of considerations,
45 And life is too much like a pathless wood
Where your face burns and tickles with the cobwebs
Broken across it, and one eye is weeping
From a twig's having lashed across it open.
I'd like to get away from earth awhile
50 And then come back to it and begin over.
May no fate willfully misunderstand me
And half grant what I wish and snatch me away
Not to return. Earth's the right place for love:
I don't know where it's likely to go better.
55 I'd like to go by climbing a birch tree,
And climb black branches up a snow-white trunk
Toward heaven, till the tree could bear no more,
But dipped its top and set me down again.
That would be good both going and coming back.
60 One could do worse than be a swinger of birches.

PEA BRUSH

I walked down alone Sunday after church
    To the place where John has been cutting trees
To see for myself about the birch
    He said I could have to bush my peas.

5 The sun in the new-cut narrow gap
    Was hot enough for the first of May,
And stifling hot with the odor of sap
    From stumps still bleeding their life away.

The frogs that were peeping a thousand shrill
10   Wherever the ground was low and wet,
The minute they heard my step went still
    To watch me and see what I came to get.

Birch boughs enough piled everywhere!—
    All fresh and sound from the recent axe.
15 Time someone came with cart and pair
    And got them off the wild flower's backs.

They might be good for garden things
    To curl a little finger round,
The same as you seize cat's-cradle strings,
20   And lift themselves up off the ground.

Small good to anything growing wild,
    They were crooking many a trillium
That had budded before the boughs were piled
    And since it was coming up had to come.

PUTTING IN THE SEED

You come to fetch me from my work to-night
When supper's on the table, and we'll see
If I can leave off burying the white
Soft petals fallen from the apple tree.
5 (Soft petals, yes, but not so barren quite,
Mingled with these, smooth bean and wrinkled pea;)
And go along with you ere you lose sight
Of what you came for and become like me,
Slave to a springtime passion for the earth.
10 How Love burns through the Putting in the Seed
On through the watching for that early birth
When, just as the soil tarnishes with weed,

The sturdy seedling with arched body comes
Shouldering its way and shedding the earth crumbs.

A Time to Talk

When a friend calls to me from the road
And slows his horse to a meaning walk,
I don't stand still and look around
On all the hills I haven't hoed,
And shout from where I am, What is it?
No, not as there is a time to talk.
I thrust my hoe in the mellow ground,
Blade-end up and five feet tall,
And plod: I go up to the stone wall
For a friendly visit.

THE COW IN APPLE TIME

Something inspires the only cow of late
To make no more of a wall than an open gate,
And think no more of wall-builders than fools.
Her face is flecked with pomace and she drools
5   A cider syrup. Having tasted fruit,
She scorns a pasture withering to the root.
She runs from tree to tree where lie and sweeten
The windfalls spiked with stubble and worm-eaten.
She leaves them bitten when she has to fly.
10   She bellows on a knoll against the sky.
Her udder shrivels and the milk goes dry.

An Encounter

Once on the kind of day called "weather breeder,"
When the heat slowly hazes and the sun
By its own power seems to be undone,
I was half boring through, half climbing through
5   A swamp of cedar. Choked with oil of cedar
And scurf of plants, and weary and over-heated,
And sorry I ever left the road I knew,
I paused and rested on a sort of hook
That had me by the coat as good as seated,
10 And since there was no other way to look,
Looked up toward heaven, and there against the blue,
Stood over me a resurrected tree,
A tree that had been down and raised again—
A barkless spectre. He had halted too,
15 As if for fear of treading upon me.
I saw the strange position of his hands—
Up at his shoulders, dragging yellow strands
Of wire with something in it from men to men.
"You here?" I said. "Where aren't you nowadays
20 And what's the news you carry—if you know?
And tell me where you're off for—Montreal?
Me? I'm not off for anywhere at all.
Sometimes I wander out of beaten ways
Half looking for the orchid Calypso."[31]

Range-Finding

The battle rent a cobweb diamond-strung
And cut a flower beside a ground bird's nest
Before it stained a single human breast.
The stricken flower bent double and so hung.
5 And still the bird revisited her young.
A butterfly its fall had dispossessed
A moment sought in air his flower of rest,
Then lightly stooped to it and fluttering clung.
On the bare upland pasture there had spread
10 O'ernight 'twixt mullein stalks a wheel of thread
And straining cables wet with silver dew.
A sudden passing bullet shook it dry.
The indwelling spider ran to greet the fly,
But finding nothing, sullenly withdrew.

The Hill Wife

LONELINESS

(Her Word)

One ought not to have to care
    So much as you and I
Care when the birds come round the house
    To seem to say good-bye;

5 Or care so much when they come back
    With whatever it is they sing;
The truth being we are as much
    Too glad for the one thing

As we are too sad for the other here—
10   With birds that fill their breasts
But with each other and themselves
    And their built or driven nests.

HOUSE FEAR

Always—I tell you this they learned—
Always at night when they returned
To the lonely house from far away
To lamps unlighted and fire gone gray,
5 They learned to rattle the lock and key
To give whatever might chance to be
Warning and time to be off in flight:
And preferring the out- to the in-door night,
They learned to leave the house-door wide
10 Until they had lit the lamp inside.

THE SMILE

(Her Word)

I didn't like the way he went away.
That smile! It never came of being gay.
Still he smiled—did you see him?—I was sure!
Perhaps because we gave him only bread
5 And the wretch knew from that that we were poor.
Perhaps because he let us give instead
Of seizing from us as he might have seized.
Perhaps he mocked at us for being wed,
Or being very young (and he was pleased
10 To have a vision of us old and dead).
I wonder how far down the road he's got.
He's watching from the woods as like as not.

THE OFT-REPEATED DREAM

She had no saying dark enough
     For the dark pine that kept
Forever trying the window-latch
     Of the room where they slept.

5 The tireless but ineffectual hands
     That with every futile pass
Made the great tree seem as a little bird
     Before the mystery of glass!

It never had been inside the room,
10   And only one of the two
Was afraid in an oft-repeated dream
        Of what the tree might do.

THE IMPULSE

It was too lonely for her there,
        And too wild,
And since there were but two of them,
        And no child,

5   And work was little in the house,
        She was free,
And followed where he furrowed field,
        Or felled tree.

She rested on a log and tossed
10   The fresh chips,
With a song only to herself
        On her lips.

And once she went to break a bough
15   Of black alder.
She strayed so far she scarcely heard
        When he called her—

And didn't answer—didn't speak—
    Or return.
She stood, and then she ran and hid
20   In the fern.

He never found her, though he looked
    Everywhere,
And he asked at her mother's house
    Was she there.

25   Sudden and swift and light as that
    The ties gave,
And he learned of finalities
    Besides the grave.

The Bonfire

"Oh, let's go up the hill and scare ourselves,
As reckless as the best of them to-night,
By setting fire to all the brush we piled
With pitchy hands to wait for rain or snow.
Oh, let's not wait for rain to make it safe.
The pile is ours: we dragged it bough on bough
Down dark converging paths between the pines.
Let's not care what we do with it to-night.
Divide it? No! But burn it as one pile
The way we piled it. And let's be the talk
Of people brought to windows by a light
Thrown from somewhere against their wall-paper.
Rouse them all, both the free and not so free
With saying what they'd like to do to us
For what they'd better wait till we have done.
Let's all but bring to life this old volcano,
If that is what the mountain ever was—
And scare ourselves. Let wild fire loose we will. . . ."

"And scare you too?" the children said together.

"Why wouldn't it scare me to have a fire
Begin in smudge with ropy smoke and know
That still, if I repent, I may recall it,
But in a moment not: a little spurt
Of burning fatness, and then nothing but
The fire itself can put it out, and that
By burning out, and before it burns out
It will have roared first and mixed sparks with stars,
And sweeping round it with a flaming sword,
Made the dim trees stand back in wider circle—
Done so much and I know not how much more

I mean it shall not do if I can bind it.
Well if it doesn't with its draft bring on
A wind to blow in earnest from some quarter,
As once it did with me upon an April.
35   The breezes were so spent with winter blowing
They seemed to fail the bluebirds under them
Short of the perch their languid flight was toward;
And my flame made a pinnacle to heaven
As I walked once round it in possession.
40   But the wind out of doors—you know the saying.
There came a gust. You used to think the trees
Made wind by fanning since you never knew
It blow but that you saw the trees in motion.
Something or someone watching made that gust.
45   It put the flame tip-down and dabbed the grass
Of over-winter with the least tip-touch
Your tongue gives salt or sugar in your hand.
The place it reached to blackened instantly.
The black was all there was by day-light,
50   That and the merest curl of cigarette smoke—
And a flame slender as the hepaticas,
Blood-root, and violets so soon to be now.
But the black spread like black death on the ground,
And I think the sky darkened with a cloud
55   Like winter and evening coming on together.
There were enough things to be thought of then.
Where the field stretches toward the north
And setting sun to Hyla brook, I gave it
To flames without twice thinking, where it verges
60   Upon the road, to flames too, though in fear
They might find fuel there, in withered brake,
Grass its full length, old silver golden-rod,

And alder and grape vine entanglement,
To leap the dusty deadline. For my own
65 I took what front there was beside. I knelt
And thrust hands in and held my face away.
Fight such a fire by rubbing not by beating.
A board is the best weapon if you have it.
I had my coat. And oh, I knew, I knew,
70 And said out loud, I couldn't bide the smother
And heat so close in; but the thought of all
The woods and town on fire by me, and all
The town turned out to fight for me—that held me.
I trusted the brook barrier, but feared
75 The road would fail; and on that side the fire
Died not without a noise of crackling wood—
Of something more than tinder-grass and weed—
That brought me to my feet to hold it back
By leaning back myself, as if the reins
80 Were round my neck and I was at the plough.
I won! But I'm sure no one ever spread
Another color over a tenth the space
That I spread coal-black over in the time
It took me. Neighbors coming home from town
85 Couldn't believe that so much black had come there
While they had backs turned, that it hadn't been there
When they had passed an hour or so before
Going the other way and they not seen it.
They looked about for someone to have done it.
90 But there was no one. I was somewhere wondering
Where all my weariness had gone and why
I walked so light on air in heavy shoes
In spite of a scorched Fourth-of-July feeling.
Why wouldn't I be scared remembering that?"

95   "If it scares you, what will it do to us?"

      "Scare you. But if you shrink from being scared,
      What would you say to war if it should come?
      That's what for reasons I should like to know—
      If you can comfort me by any answer."

100   "Oh, but war's not for children—it's for men."

      "Now we are digging almost down to China.
      My dears, my dears, you thought that—we all thought it.
      So your mistake was ours. Haven't you heard, though,
      About the ships where war has found them out
105   At sea, about the towns where war has come
      Through opening clouds at night with droning speed
      Further o'erhead than all but stars and angels,—
      And children in the ships and in the towns?
      Haven't you heard what we have lived to learn?
110   Nothing so new—something we had forgotten:
      War is for everyone, for children too.
      I wasn't going to tell you and I mustn't.
      The best way is to come up hill with me
      And have our fire and laugh and be afraid."

A Girl's Garden

A neighbor of mine in the village
   Likes to tell how one spring
When she was a girl on the farm, she did
   A childlike thing.

5 One day she asked her father
   To give her a garden plot
To plant and tend and reap herself,
   And he said, "Why not?"

In casting about for a corner
10   He thought of an idle bit
Of walled-off ground where a shop had stood,
   And he said, "Just it."

And he said, "That ought to make you
   An ideal one-girl farm,
15 And give you a chance to put some strength
   On your slim-jim arm."

It was not enough of a garden,
   Her father said, to plough;
So she had to work it all by hand,
20   But she don't mind now.

She wheeled the dung in the wheelbarrow
   Along a stretch of road;
But she always ran away and left
   Her not-nice load.

25 And hid from anyone passing.
   And then she begged the seed.

She says she thinks she planted one
    Of all things but weed.

A hill each of potatoes,
30   Radishes, lettuce, peas,
Tomatoes, beets, beans, pumpkins, corn,
    And even fruit trees

And yes, she has long mistrusted
    That a cider apple tree
35 In bearing there to-day is hers,
    Or at least may be.

Her crop was a miscellany
    When all was said and done,
A little bit of everything,
40   A great deal of none.

Now when she sees in the village
    How village things go,
Just when it seems to come in right,
    She says, "*I* know!

45 It's as when I was a farmer——"
    Oh, never by way of advice!
And she never sins by telling the tale
    To the same person twice.

The Exposed Nest

You were forever finding some new play.
So when I saw you down on hands and knees
In the meadow, busy with the new-cut hay,
Trying, I thought, to set it up on end,
5 I went to show you how to make it stay,
If that was your idea, against the breeze,
And, if you asked me, even help pretend
To make it root again and grow afresh.
But 'twas no make-believe with you to-day,
10 Nor was the grass itself your real concern,
Though I found your hand full of wilted fern,
Steel-bright June-grass, and blackening heads of clover.
'Twas a nest full of young birds on the ground
The cutter-bar had just gone champing over
15 (Miraculously without tasting flesh)
And left defenseless to the heat and light.
You wanted to restore them to their right
Of something interposed between their sight
And too much world at once—could means be found.
20 The way the nest-full every time we stirred
Stood up to us as to a mother-bird
Whose coming home has been too long deferred,
Made me ask would the mother-bird return
And care for them in such a change of scene
25 And might our meddling make her more afraid.
That was a thing we could not wait to learn.
We saw the risk we took in doing good,
But dared not spare to do the best we could
Though harm should come of it; so built the screen
30 You had begun, and gave them back their shade.
All this to prove we cared. Why is there then
No more to tell? We turned to other things.

I haven't any memory—have you?—
35 Of ever coming to the place again
To see if the birds lived the first night through,
And so at last to learn to use their wings.

"OUT, OUT—"[32]

The buzz-saw snarled and rattled in the yard
And made dust and dropped stove-length sticks of wood,
Sweet-scented stuff when the breeze drew across it.
And from there those that lifted eyes could count
5   Five mountain ranges one behind the other
Under the sunset far into Vermont.
And the saw snarled and rattled, snarled and rattled,
As it ran light, or had to bear a load.
And nothing happened: day was all but done.
10 Call it a day, I wish they might have said
To please the boy by giving him the half hour
That a boy counts so much when saved from work.
His sister stood beside them in her apron
To tell them "Supper." At the word, the saw,
15 As if to prove saws knew what supper meant,
Leaped out at the boy's hand, or seemed to leap—
He must have given the hand. However it was,
Neither refused the meeting. But the hand!
The boy's first outcry was a rueful laugh,
20 As he swung toward them holding up the hand
Half in appeal, but half as if to keep
The life from spilling. Then the boy saw all—
Since he was old enough to know, big boy
Doing a man's work, though a child at heart—

25

The doctor, when he comes. Don't let him, sister!"
So. But the hand was gone already.
The doctor put him in the dark of ether.
He lay and puffed his lips out with his breath.
30 And then—the watcher at his pulse took fright.

No one believed. They listened at his heart.
Little—less—nothing!—and that ended it.
No more to build on there. And they, since they
Were not the one dead, turned to their affairs.

BROWN'S DESCENT
or
The Willy-Nilly Slide

Brown lived at such a lofty farm
    That everyone for miles could see
His lantern when he did his chores
    In winter after half-past three.

5 And many must have seen him make
    His wild descent from there one night,
'Cross lots, 'cross walls, 'cross everything,
    Describing rings of lantern light.

Between the house and barn the gale
10   Got him by something he had on
And blew him out on the icy crust
    That cased the world, and he was gone!

Walls were all buried, trees were few:
    He saw no stay unless he stove
15 A hole in somewhere with his heel.
    But though repeatedly he strove

And stamped and said things to himself,
    And sometimes something seemed to yield,
He gained no foothold, but pursued
20   His journey down from field to field.

Sometimes he came with arms outspread
    Like wings, revolving in the scene
Upon his longer axis, and
    With no small dignity of mien.

25 Faster or slower as he chanced,
    Sitting or standing as he chose,
According as he feared to risk
    His neck, or thought to spare his clothes,

He never let the lantern drop.
30   And some exclaimed who saw afar
The figures he described with it,
    "I wonder what those signals are

Brown makes at such an hour of night!
    He's celebrating something strange.
35 I wonder if he's sold his farm,
    Or been made Master of the Grange."

He reeled, he lurched, he bobbed, he checked;
    He fell and made the lantern rattle
(But saved the light from going out.)
40   So half-way down he fought the battle

Incredulous of his own bad luck.
    And then becoming reconciled
To everything, he gave it up
    And came down like a coasting child.

45 "Well—I—be—" that was all he said,
    As standing in the river road,
He looked back up the slippery slope
    (Two miles it was) to his abode.

Sometimes as an authority
50   On motor-cars, I'm asked if I

Should say our stock was petered out,
  And this is my sincere reply:

Yankees are what they always were.
  Don't think Brown ever gave up hope
55 Of getting home again because
  He couldn't climb that slippery slope;

Or even thought of standing there
  Until the January thaw
Should take the polish off the crust.
60 He bowed with grace to natural law,

And then went round it on his feet,
  After the manner of our stock;
Not much concerned for those to whom,
  At that particular time o'clock,

65 It must have looked as if the course
  He steered was really straight away
From that which he was headed for—
  Not much concerned for them, I say:

No more so than became a man—
70 *And* politician at odd seasons.
I've kept Brown standing in the cold
  While I invested him with reasons;

But now he snapped his eyes three times;
  Then shook his lantern, saying, "Ile's
75 'Bout out!" and took the long way home
  By road, a matter of several miles.

THE GUM-GATHERER

There overtook me and drew me in
To his down-hill, early-morning stride,
And set me five miles on my road
Better than if he had had me ride,
5 A man with a swinging bag for load
And half the bag wound round his hand.
We talked like barking above the din
Of water we walked along beside.
And for my telling him where I'd been
10 And where I lived in mountain land
To be coming home the way I was,
He told me a little about himself.
He came from higher up in the pass
Where the grist of the new-beginning brooks
15 Is blocks split off the mountain mass—
And hopeless grist enough it looks
Ever to grind to soil for grass.
(The way it is will do for moss.)
There he had built his stolen shack.
20 It had to be a stolen shack
Because of the fears of fire and loss
That trouble the sleep of lumber folk:
Visions of half the world burned black
And the sun shrunken yellow in smoke.
25 We know who when they come to town
Bring berries under the wagon seat,
Or a basket of eggs between their feet;
What this man brought in a cotton sack
Was gum, the gum of the mountain spruce.
30 He showed me lumps of the scented stuff
Like uncut jewels, dull and rough.

It comes to market golden brown;
But turns to pink between the teeth.

I told him this is a pleasant life
35   To set your breast to the bark of trees
That all your days are dim beneath,
And reaching up with a little knife,
To loose the resin and take it down
And bring it to market when you please.

The Line-Gang

Here come the line-gang pioneering by.
They throw a forest down less cut than broken.
They plant dead trees for living, and the dead
They string together with a living thread.
5   They string an instrument against the sky
Wherein words whether beaten out or spoken
Will run as hushed as when they were a thought.
But in no hush they string it: they go past
With shouts afar to pull the cable taut,
10   To hold it hard until they make it fast,
To ease away—they have it. With a laugh,
An oath of towns that set the wild at naught
They bring the telephone and telegraph.

THE VANISHING RED

He is said to have been the last Red Man
In Acton. And the Miller is said to have laughed—
If you like to call such a sound a laugh.
But he gave no one else a laughter's license.
5   For he turned suddenly grave as if to say,
"Whose business,—if I take it on myself,
Whose business—but why talk round the barn?—
When it's just that I hold with getting a thing done with."
You can't get back and see it as he saw it.
10 It's too long a story to go into now.
You'd have to have been there and lived it.
Then you wouldn't have looked on it as just a matter
Of who began it between the two races.

Some guttural exclamation of surprise
15 The Red Man gave in poking about the mill
Over the great big thumping shuffling mill-stone
Disgusted the Miller physically as coming
From one who had no right to be heard from.
"Come, John," he said, "you want to see the wheel pit?"

20 He took him down below a cramping rafter,
And showed him, through a manhole in the floor,
The water in desperate straits like frantic fish,
Salmon and sturgeon, lashing with their tails.
Then he shut down the trap door with a ring in it
25 That jangled even above the general noise,
And came up stairs alone—and gave that laugh,
And said something to a man with a meal-sack
That the man with the meal-sack didn't catch—then.
Oh, yes, he showed John the wheel pit all right.

SNOW

The three stood listening to a fresh access
Of wind that caught against the house a moment,
Gulped snow, and then blew free again—the Coles
Dressed, but dishevelled from some hours of sleep,
5   Meserve belittled in the great skin coat he wore.

Meserve was first to speak. He pointed backward
Over his shoulder with his pipe-stem, saying,
"You can just see it glancing off the roof
Making a great scroll upward toward the sky,
10 Long enough for recording all our names on.—
I think I'll just call up my wife and tell her
I'm here—so far—and starting on again.
I'll call her softly so that if she's wise
And gone to sleep, she needn't wake to answer."
15 Three times he barely stirred the bell, then listened.
"Why, Lett, still up? Lett, I'm at Cole's. I'm late.
I called you up to say Good-night from here
Before I went to say Good-morning there.—
I thought I would.— I know, but, Lett—I know—
20 I could, but what's the sense? The rest won't be
So bad.— Give me an hour for it.— Ho, ho,
Three hours to here! But that was all up hill;
The rest is down.— Why no, no, not a wallow:
They kept their heads and took their time to it
25 Like darlings, both of them. They're in the barn.—
My dear, I'm coming just the same. I didn't
Call you to ask you to invite me home.—"
He lingered for some word she wouldn't say,
Said it at last himself, "Good-night," and then,
30 Getting no answer, closed the telephone.
The three stood in the lamplight round the table

With lowered eyes a moment till he said,
"I'll just see how the horses are."

                              "Yes, do,"
Both the Coles said together. Mrs. Cole
35 Added: "You can judge better after seeing.—
I want you here with me, Fred. Leave him here,
Brother Meserve. You know to find your way
Out through the shed."

                              "I guess I know my way,
I guess I know where I can find my name
40 Carved in the shed to tell me who I am
If it don't tell me where I am. I used
To play—"

                    "You tend your horses and come back.
Fred Cole, you're going to let him!"

                                        "Well, aren't you?
How can you help yourself?"

                                  "I called him Brother.
45 Why did I call him that?"

                              "It's right enough.
That's all you ever heard him called round here.
He seems to have lost off his Christian name."

"Christian enough I should call that myself.
He took no notice, did he? Well, at least
50 I didn't use it out of love of him,

The dear knows. I detest the thought of him
With his ten children under ten years old.
I hate his wretched little Racker Sect,[33]
All's ever I heard of it, which isn't much.
55   But that's not saying—Look, Fred Cole, it's twelve,
Isn't it, now? He's been here half an hour.
He says he left the village store at nine.
Three hours to do four miles—a mile an hour
Or not much better. Why, it doesn't seem
60   As if a man could move that slow and move.
Try to think what he did with all that time.
And three miles more to go!"

                         "Don't let him go.
Stick to him, Helen. Make him answer you.
That sort of man talks straight on all his life
65   From the last thing he said himself, stone deaf
To anything anyone else may say.
I should have thought, though, you could make him hear
      you."

"What is he doing out a night like this?
Why can't he stay at home?"

                         "He had to preach."

"It's no night to be out."

70   "He may be small,
He may be good, but one thing's sure, he's tough."

"And strong of stale tobacco."

- 188 -

                              "He'll pull through."

"You only say so. Not another house
Or shelter to put into from this place
75 To theirs. I'm going to call his wife again."

"Wait and he may. Let's see what he will do.
Let's see if he will think of her again.
But then I doubt he's thinking of himself
He doesn't look on it as anything."

"He shan't go—there!"

80   "It *is* a night, my dear."

"One thing: he didn't drag God into it."

"He don't consider it a case for God."

"You think so, do you? You don't know the kind.
He's getting up a miracle this minute.
85 Privately—to himself, right now, he's thinking
He'll make a case of it if he succeeds,
But keep still if he fails."

                              "Keep still all over.
He'll be dead—dead and buried."

                              "Such a trouble!
Not but I've every reason not to care
90 What happens to him if it only takes

Some of the sanctimonious conceit
Out of one of those pious scalawags."

"Nonsense to that! You want to see him safe."

"You like the runt."

        "Don't you a little?"

                "Well,
95 I don't like what he's doing, which is what
You like, and like him for."

          "Oh, yes you do.
You like your fun as well as anyone;
Only you women have to put these airs on
To impress men. You've got us so ashamed
100 Of being men we can't look at a good fight
Between two boys and not feel bound to stop it.
Let the man freeze an ear or two, I say.—
He's here. I leave him all to you. Go in
And save his life.— All right, come in, Meserve.
105 Sit down, sit down. How did you find the horses?"

"Fine, fine."

        "And ready for some more? My wife here
Says it won't do. You've got to give it up."

"Won't you to please me? Please! If I say please?
Mr. Meserve, I'll leave it to *your* wife.
110 What *did* your wife say on the telephone?"

Meserve seemed to heed nothing but the lamp
Or something not far from it on the table.
By straightening out and lifting a forefinger,
He pointed with his hand from where it lay
Like a white crumpled spider on his knee:
"That leaf there in your open book! It moved
Just then, I thought. It's stood erect like that,
There on the table, ever since I came,
Trying to turn itself backward or forward,
I've had my eye on it to make out which;
If forward, then it's with a friend's impatience—
You see I know—to get you on to things
It wants to see how you will take, if backward
It's from regret for something you have passed
And failed to see the good of. Never mind,
Things must expect to come in front of us
A many times—I don't say just how many—
That varies with the things—before we see them.
One of the lies would make it out that nothing
Ever presents itself before us twice.
Where would we be at last if that were so?
Our very life depends on everything's
Recurring till we answer from within.
The thousandth time may prove the charm.— That leaf!
It can't turn either way. It needs the wind's help.
But the wind didn't move it if it moved.
It moved itself. The wind's at naught in here.
It couldn't stir so sensitively poised
A thing as that. It couldn't reach the lamp
To get a puff of black smoke from the flame,
Or blow a rumple in the collie's coat.
You make a little foursquare block of air,

Quiet and light and warm, in spite of all
The illimitable dark and cold and storm,
145 And by so doing give these three, lamp, dog,
And book-leaf, that keep near you, their repose;
Though for all anyone can tell, repose
May be the thing you haven't, yet you give it.
So false it is that what we haven't we can't give;
150 So false, that what we always say is true.
I'll have to turn the leaf if no one else will.
It won't lie down. Then let it stand. Who cares?"

"I shouldn't want to hurry you, Meserve,
But if you're going— Say you'll stay, you know?
155 But let me raise this curtain on a scene,
And show you how it's piling up against you.
You see the snow-white through the white of frost?
Ask Helen how far up the sash it's climbed
Since last we read the gage."

                              "It looks as if
160 Some pallid thing had squashed its features flat
And its eyes shut with overeagerness
To see what people found so interesting
In one another, and had gone to sleep
Of its own stupid lack of understanding,
165 Or broken its white neck of mushroom stuff
Short off, and died against the window-pane."

"Brother Meserve, take care, you'll scare yourself
More than you will us with such nightmare talk.
It's you it matters to, because it's you
170 Who have to go out into it alone."

"Let him talk, Helen, and perhaps he'll stay."

"Before you drop the curtain—I'm reminded:
You recollect the boy who came out here
To breathe the air one winter—had a room
175 Down at the Averys'? Well, one sunny morning
After a downy storm, he passed our place
And found me banking up the house with snow.
And I was burrowing in deep for warmth,
Piling it well above the window-sills.
180 The snow against the window caught his eye.
'Hey, that's a pretty thought'—those were his words.
'So you can think it's six feet deep outside,
While you sit warm and read up balanced rations.
You can't get too much winter in the winter.'
185 Those were his words. And he went home and all
But banked the daylight out of Avery's windows.
Now you and I would go to no such length.
At the same time you can't deny it makes
It not a mite worse, sitting here, we three,
190 Playing our fancy, to have the snowline run
So high across the pane outside. There where
There is a sort of tunnel in the frost
More like a tunnel than a hole—way down
At the far end of it you see a stir
195 And quiver like the frayed edge of the drift
Blown in the wind. I *like* that—I like *that*.
Well, now I leave you, people."

                                "Come, Meserve,
We thought you were deciding not to go—
The ways you found to say the praise of comfort
200 And being where you are. You want to stay."

"I'll own it's cold for such a fall of snow.
This house is frozen brittle, all except
This room you sit in. If you think the wind
Sounds further off, it's not because it's dying;
You're further under in the snow—that's all—
And feel it less. Hear the soft bombs of dust
It bursts against us at the chimney mouth,
And at the eaves. I like it from inside
More than I shall out in it. But the horses
Are rested and it's time to say good-night,
And let you get to bed again. Good-night,
Sorry I had to break in on your sleep."

"Lucky for you you did. Lucky for you
You had us for a half-way station
To stop at. If you were the kind of man
Paid heed to women, you'd take my advice
And for your family's sake stay where you are.
But what good is my saying it over and over?
You've done more than you had a right to think
You could do—*now*. You know the risk you take
In going on."

                    "Our snow-storms as a rule
Aren't looked on as man-killers, and although
I'd rather be the beast that sleeps the sleep
Under it all, his door sealed up and lost,
Than the man fighting it to keep above it,
Yet think of the small birds at roost and not
In nests. Shall I be counted less than they are?
Their bulk in water would be frozen rock
In no time out to-night. And yet to-morrow

- 194 -

230 They will come budding boughs from tree to tree
Flirting their wings and saying Chickadee,[34]
As if not knowing what you meant by the word storm."

"But why when no one wants you to go on?
Your wife—she doesn't want you to. We don't,
235 And you yourself don't want to. Who else is there?"

"Save us from being cornered by a woman.
Well, there's"—She told Fred afterward that in
The pause right there, she thought the dreaded word
Was coming, "God." But no, he only said
240 "Well, there's—the storm. That says I must go on.
That wants me as a war might if it came.
Ask any man."

                    He threw her that as something
To last her till he got outside the door.
He had Cole with him to the barn to see him off.
245 When Cole returned he found his wife still standing
Beside the table near the open book,
Not reading it.

                    "Well, what kind of a man
Do you call that?" she said.

                              "He had the gift
Of words, or is it tongues,[35] I ought to say?"

250 "Was ever such a man for seeing likeness?"

"Or disregarding people's civil questions—
What? We've found out in one hour more about him
Than we had seeing him pass by in the road
A thousand times. If that's the way he preaches!
You didn't think you'd keep him after all.
Oh, I'm not blaming you. He didn't leave you
Much say in the matter, and I'm just as glad
We're not in for a night of him. No sleep
If he had stayed. The least thing set him going.
It's quiet as an empty church without him."

"But how much better off are we as it is?
We'll have to sit here till we know he's safe."

"Yes, I suppose you'll want to, but I shouldn't.
He knows what he can do, or he wouldn't try.
Get into bed I say, and get some rest.
He won't come back, and if he telephones,
It won't be for an hour or two."

                                    "Well then.
We can't be any help by sitting here
And living his fight through with him, I suppose."

Cole had been telephoning in the dark.
Mrs. Cole's voice came from an inner room:
"Did she call you or you call her?"

                              "She me.
You'd better dress: you won't go back to bed.
We must have been asleep: it's three and after."

275 "Had she been ringing long? I'll get my wrapper.
I want to speak to her."

                    "All she said was,
He hadn't come and had he really started."

"She knew he had, poor thing, two hours ago."

"He had the shovel. He'll have made a fight."

280 "Why did I ever let him leave this house!"

"Don't begin that. You did the best you could
To keep him—though perhaps you didn't quite
Conceal a wish to see him show the spunk
To disobey you. Much his wife'll thank you."

285 "Fred, after all I said! You shan't make out
That it was any way but what it was.
Did she let on by any word she said
She didn't thank me?"

                    "When I told her 'Gone,'
'Well then,' she said, and 'Well then'—like a threat.
290 And then her voice came scraping slow: 'Oh, you,
Why did you let him go'?"

                    "Asked why we let him?
You let me there. I'll ask her why she let him.
She didn't dare to speak when he was here.
Their number's—twenty-one? The thing won't work.
295 Someone's receiver's down. The handle stumbles.

The stubborn thing, the way it jars your arm!
It's theirs. She's dropped it from her hand and gone."

"Try speaking. Say 'Hello'!"

        "Hello. Hello."

"What do you hear?"

        "I hear an empty room—

300 You know—it sounds that way. And yes, I hear—
I think I hear a clock—and windows rattling.
No step though. If she's there she's sitting down."

"Shout, she may hear you."

        "Shouting is no good."

335 "Keep speaking then."

        "Hello. Hello. Hello.
305 You don't suppose—? She wouldn't go out doors?"

"I'm half afraid that's just what she might do."

"And leave the children?"

        "Wait and call again.
You can't hear whether she has left the door
Wide open and the wind's blown out the lamp
310 And the fire's died and the room's dark and cold?"

"One of two things, either she's gone to bed
Or gone out doors."

                              "In which case both are lost.
Do you know what she's like? Have you ever met her?
It's strange she doesn't want to speak to us."

315   "Fred, see if you can hear what I hear. Come."

"A clock maybe."

                              "Don't you hear something else?"

"Not talking."

                    "No."

                              "Why, yes, I hear—what is it?"

"What do you say it is?"

                              "A baby's crying!
Frantic it sounds, though muffled and far off.
320   Its mother wouldn't let it cry like that,
Not if she's there."

                              "What do you make of it?"

"There's only one thing possible to make,
That is, assuming—that she has gone out.

Of course she hasn't though." They both sat down
Helpless. "There's nothing we can do till morning."

"Fred, I shan't let you think of going out."

"Hold on." The double bell began to chirp.
They started up. Fred took the telephone.
"Hello, Meserve. You're there, then!—And your wife?

Good! Why I asked—she didn't seem to answer.
He says she went to let him in the barn.—
We're glad. Oh, say no more about it, man.
Drop in and see us when you're passing."

                                    "Well,
She has him then, though what she wants him for
I *don't* see."

                    "Possibly not for herself.
Maybe she only wants him for the children."

"The whole to-do seems to have been for nothing.
What spoiled our night was to him just his fun.
What did he come in for?—To talk and visit?
Thought he'd just call to tell us it was snowing.
If he thinks he is going to make our house
A halfway coffee house 'twixt town and nowhere——"

"I thought you'd feel you'd been too much concerned."

"You think you haven't been concerned yourself."

345 "If you mean he was inconsiderate
To rout us out to think for him at midnight
And then take our advice no more than nothing,
Why, I agree with you. But let's forgive him.
We've had a share in one night of his life.
350 What'll you bet he ever calls again?"

THE SOUND OF THE TREES

I wonder about the trees.
Why do we wish to bear
Forever the noise of these
More than another noise
So close to our dwelling place?
We suffer them by the day
Till we lose all measure of pace,
And fixity in our joys,
And acquire a listening air.
They are that that talks of going
But never gets away;
And that talks no less for knowing,
As it grows wiser and older,
That now it means to stay.
My feet tug at the floor
And my head sways to my shoulder
Sometimes when I watch trees sway,
From the window or the door.
I shall set forth for somewhere,
I shall make the reckless choice
Some day when they are in voice
And tossing so as to scare
The white clouds over them on.
I shall have less to say,
But I shall be gone.

POEMS TO 1922
(LATER PUBLISHED IN
NEW HAMPSHIRE)

A STAR IN A STONE-BOAT[36]

Never tell me that not one star of all
That slip from heaven at night and softly fall
Has been picked up with stones to build a wall.

Some laborer found one faded and stone cold,
5   And saving that its weight suggested gold,
And tugged it from his first too certain hold,

He noticed nothing in it to remark.
He was not used to handling stars thrown dark
And lifeless from an interrupted arc.

10   He did not recognize in that smooth coal
The one thing palpable beside the soul
To penetrate the air in which we roll.

He did not see how like a flying thing
It brooded ant-eggs, and had one large wing,
15   One not so large for flying in a ring,

And a long Bird of Paradise's tail,[37]
(Though these when not in use to fly and trail
It drew back in its body like a snail);

Nor know that he might move it from the spot,
20   The harm was done; from having been star-shot
The very nature of the soil was hot

And burning to yield flowers instead of grain,
Flowers fanned and not put out by all the rain
Poured on them by his prayers prayed in vain.

25 He moved it roughly with an iron bar,
He loaded an old stone-boat with the star
And not, as you might think, a flying car,

Such as even poets would admit perforce
More practical than Pegasus the horse
30 If it could put a star back in its course.

He dragged it through the plowed ground at a pace
But faintly reminiscent of the race
Of jostling rock in interstellar space.

It went for building stone, and I, as though
35 Commanded in a dream, forever go
To right the wrong that this should have been so.

Yet ask where else it could have gone as well,
I do not know—I cannot stop to tell:
He might have left it lying where it fell.

40 From following walls I never lift my eye
Except at night to places in the sky
Where showers of charted meteors let fly.

Some may know what they seek in school and church,
And why they seek it there; for what I search
45 I must go measuring stone walls, perch on perch;

Sure that though not a star of death and birth,
So not to be compared, perhaps, in worth
To such resorts of life as Mars and Earth,

Though not, I say, a star of death and sin,
50 It yet has poles, and only needs a spin
To show its worldly nature and begin

To chafe and shuffle in my calloused palm
And run off in strange tangents with my arm
As fish do with the line in first alarm.

55 Such as it is, it promises the prize
Of the one world complete in any size
That I am like to compass, fool or wise.

THE CENSUS-TAKER

I came an errand one cloud-blowing evening
To a slab-built, black-paper-covered house
Of one room and one window and one door,
The only dwelling in a waste cut over
5   A hundred square miles round it in the mountains:
And that not dwelt in now by men or women.
(It never had been dwelt in, though, by women,
So what is this I make a sorrow of?)
I came as census-taker to the waste
10   To count the people in it and found none,
None in the hundred miles, none in the house,
Where I came last with some hope, but not much
After hours' overlooking from the cliffs
An emptiness flayed to the very stone.
15   I found no people that dared show themselves,
None not in hiding from the outward eye.
The time was autumn, but how anyone
Could tell the time of year when every tree
That could have dropped a leaf was down itself
20   And nothing but the stump of it was left
Now bringing out its rings in sugar of pitch;
And every tree up stood a rotting trunk
Without a single leaf to spend on autumn,
Or branch to whistle after what was spent.
25   Perhaps the wind the more without the help
Of breathing trees said something of the time
Of year or day the way it swung a door
Forever off the latch, as if rude men
Passed in and slammed it shut each one behind him
30   For the next one to open for himself.
I counted nine I had no right to count
(But this was dreamy unofficial counting)

Before I made the tenth across the threshold.
Where was my supper? Where was anyone's?
35 No lamp was lit. Nothing was on the table.
The stove was cold—the stove was off the chimney—
And down by one side where it lacked a leg.
The people that had loudly passed the door
Were people to the ear but not the eye.
40 They were not on the table with their elbows.
They were not sleeping in the shelves of bunks.
I saw no men there and no bones of men there.
I armed myself against such bones as might be
With the pitch-blackened stub of an ax-handle
45 I picked up off the straw-dust covered floor.
Not bones, but the ill-fitted window rattled.
The door was still because I held it shut
While I thought what to do that could be done—
About the house—about the people not there.
50 The house in one year fallen to decay
Filled me with no less sorrow than the houses
Fallen to ruin in ten thousand years
Where Asia wedges Africa from Europe.
Nothing was left to do that I could see
55 Unless to find that there was no one there
And declare to the cliffs too far for echo,
"The place is desert and let whoso lurks
In silence, if in this he be aggrieved,
Break silence now or be forever silent.
60 Let him say why it should not be declared so."
The melancholy of having to count souls
Where they grow fewer and fewer every year
Is extreme where they shrink to none at all.
It must be I want life to go on living.

MAPLE

Her teacher's certainty it must be Mabel
Made Maple first take notice of her name.
She asked her father and he told her "Maple—
Maple is right."

             "But teacher told the school
5 There's no such name."

                 "Teachers don't know as much
As fathers about children, you tell teacher.
You tell her that it's M-A-P-L-E.
You ask her if she knows a maple tree.
Well, you were named after a maple tree.
10 Your mother named you. You and she just saw
Each other in passing in the room upstairs,
One coming this way into life, and one
Going the other out of life—you know?
So you can't have much recollection of her.
15 She had been having a long look at you.
She put her finger in your cheek so hard
It must have made your dimple there, and said,
'Maple.' I said it too: 'Yes, for her name.'
She nodded. So we're sure there's no mistake.
20 I don't know what she wanted it to mean,
But it seems like some word she left to bid you
Be a good girl—be like a maple tree.
How like a maple tree's for us to guess.
Or for a little girl to guess sometime.
25 Not now—at least I shouldn't try too hard now.
By and by I will tell you all I know
About the different trees, and something, too,

About your mother that perhaps may help."
Dangerous self-arousing words to sow
30 In a child's mind, he suddenly perceived.
Luckily all she wanted of her name then
Was to rebuke her teacher with it next day,
And give the teacher a scare as from her father.
Anything further had been wasted on her,
35 Or so he'd tried to think to avoid blame.
She would forget it. She all but forgot it.
What he'd sowed with her slept so long a sleep,
And came so near death in the dark of years,
That when it woke and came to life again
40 The flower was different from the parent seed.
It came back vaguely at the glass one day,
As she stood saying over her name aloud,
Striking it gently across her lowered eyes
To make it go well with the way she looked.
45 What was it about the name? She saw its strangeness
Lay in its having meaning. Other names,
As Lesley, Carol, Irma, Marjorie,
Signified nothing. Rose could have a meaning,
But hadn't as it went. (She knew a Rose.)
50 This difference from other names it was
Made people notice it—and notice her.
(They either noticed it, or got it wrong.)
The problem was to find out what it asked
In dress or manner of the girl who bore it.
55 If she could form some notion of her mother—
What she had thought was lovely, and what good.
This was her mother's childhood home;
The house one story high in front, three stories

On the end it presented to the road.
60 (The arrangement made a pleasant sunny cellar.)
Her mother's bedroom was her father's still,
Where she could watch her mother's picture fading.
Once she found for a bookmark in the Bible
A maple leaf she thought must have been laid
65 In wait for her there. She read every word
Of the two pages it was pressed between
As if it was her mother speaking to her.
She forgot to put back the leaf in closing
And lost the place never to find again.
70 She was sure, though, there had been nothing in it.

So she looked for herself, as everyone
Looks for himself, more or less outwardly.
And her self-seeking, fitful though it was,
May still have been what led her on to read,
75 And think a little, and get some city schooling.
She learned shorthand, whatever shorthand may
Have had to do with it—she sometimes wondered.
So, till she found herself in a strange place
For the name Maple to have brought her to,
80 Taking dictation on a paper pad,
And in the pauses when she raised her eyes
Watching out of a nineteenth story window
An airship laboring with unship-like motion
And a vague all-disturbing roar above the river
85 Beyond the highest city built with hands.
Someone was saying in such natural tones
She almost wrote the words down on her knee.

"Do you know you remind me of a tree—
A maple tree?"

        "Because my name is Maple?"

90   "Isn't it Mabel? I thought it was Mabel."

"No doubt you've heard the office call me Mabel.
I have to let them call me what they like."

They were both stirred that he should have divined
Without the name her personal mystery.
95   It made it seem as if there must be something
She must have missed herself. So they were married,
And took the fancy home with them to live by.

They went on pilgrimage once to her father's
(The house one story high in front, three stories
100   On the end it presented to the road)
To see if there was not some special tree
She might have overlooked. They could find none,
Not so much as a single tree for shade,
Let alone grove of trees for sugar orchard.
105   She told him of the bookmark maple leaf
In the big Bible, and all she remembered
Of the place marked with it—"Wave offering,[38]
Something about wave offering, it said."

"You've never asked your father outright, have you?"

110   "I have, and been put off sometime, I think."
    (This was her faded memory of the way
    Once long ago her father had put himself off.)

    "Because no telling but it may have been
    Something between your father and your mother
115   Not meant for us at all."

                      "Not meant for me?
    Where would the fairness be in giving me
    A name to carry for life, and never know
    The secret of?"

                "And then it may have been
    Something a father couldn't tell a daughter
120   As well as could a mother. And again
    It may have been their one lapse into fancy
    'Twould be too bad to make him sorry for
    By bringing it up to him when too old.
    Your father feels us round him with our questing,
125   And holds us off unnecessarily,
    As if he didn't know what little thing
    Might lead us to a discovery.
    It was as personal as he could be
    About the way he saw it was with you
130   To say your mother, had she lived, would be
    As far again as from being born to bearing."

    "Just one look more with what you say in mind,
    And I give up"; which last look came to nothing.

But, though they now gave up the search forever,
135 They clung to what one had seen in the other
By inspiration. It proved there was something.
They kept their thoughts away from when the maples
Stood uniform in buckets, and the steam
Of sap and snow rolled off the sugar house.
140 When they made her related to the maple,
It was the tree the autumn fire ran through
And swept of leathern leaves, but left the bark
Unscorched, unblackened, even, by any smoke.
They always took their holidays in autumn.
145 Once they came on a maple in a glade,
Standing alone with smooth arms lifted up,
And every leaf of foliage she'd worn
Laid scarlet and pale pink about her feet.
But its age kept them from considering this one.
150 Twenty-five years ago at Maple's naming
It hardly could have been a two-leaved seedling
The next cow might have licked up out at pasture.
Could it have been another maple like it?
They hovered for a moment near discovery,
155 Figurative enough to see the symbol,
But lacking faith in anything to mean
The same at different times to different people.
Perhaps a filial diffidence partly kept them
From thinking it could be a thing so bridal.
160 And anyway it came too late for Maple.
She used her hands to cover up her eyes.
"We would not see the secret if we could now:
We are not looking for it any more."

Thus had a name with a meaning, given in death,
165 Made a girl's marriage, and ruled in her life.
No matter that the meaning was not clear.
A name with meaning could bring up a child,
Taking the child out of the parents' hands.
Better a meaningless name, I should say,
170 As leaving more to nature and happy chance.
Name children some names and see what you do.

THE AX-HELVE

I've known ere now an interfering branch
Of alder catch my lifted ax behind me.
But that was in the woods, to hold my hand
From striking at another alder's roots,
5   And that was, as I say, an alder branch.
This was a man, Baptiste, who stole one day
Behind me on the snow in my own yard
Where I was working at the chopping-block,
And cutting nothing not cut down already.
10 He caught my ax expertly on the rise,
When all my strength put forth was in his favor,
Held it a moment where it was, to calm me,
Then took it from me—and I let him take it.
I didn't know him well enough to know
15 What it was all about. There might be something
He had in mind to say to a bad neighbor
He might prefer to say to him disarmed.
But all he had to tell me in French-English
Was what he thought of—not me, but my ax,
20 Me only as I took my ax to heart.
It was the bad ax-helve someone had sold me—
"Made on machine," he said, plowing the grain
With a thick thumbnail to show how it ran
Across the handle's long drawn serpentine,
25 Like the two strokes across a dollar sign.
"You give her one good crack, she's snap raght off.
Den where's your hax-ead flying t'rough de hair?"
Admitted; and yet, what was that to him?

"Come on my house and I put you one in
30 What's las' awhile—good hick'ry what's grow crooked,
De second growt' I cut myself—tough, tough!"

Something to sell? That wasn't how it sounded.

"Den when you say you come? It's cost you nothing.
Tonaght?"

As well tonight as any night.

35 Beyond an over-warmth of kitchen stove
My welcome differed from no other welcome.
Baptiste knew best why I was where I was.
So long as he would leave enough unsaid,
I shouldn't mind his being overjoyed
40 (If overjoyed he was) at having got me
Where I must judge if what he knew about an ax
That not everybody else knew was to count
For nothing in the measure of a neighbor.
Hard if, though cast away for life 'mid Yankees,
45 A Frenchman couldn't get his human rating!

Mrs. Baptiste came in and rocked a chair
That had as many motions as the world:
One back and forward, in and out of shadow,
That got her nowhere; one more gradual,
50 Sideways, that would have run her on the stove
In time, had she not realized her danger
And caught herself up bodily, chair and all,
And set herself back where she started from.
"She ain't spick too much Henglish—dat's too bad."
55 I was afraid, in brightening first on me,
Then on Baptiste, as if she understood
What passed between us, she was only feigning.
Baptiste was anxious for her; but no more

Than for himself, so placed he couldn't hope
60 To keep his bargain of the morning with me
In time to keep me from suspecting him
Of really never having meant to keep it.

Needlessly soon he had his ax-helves out,
A quiverful to choose from, since he wished me
65 To have the best he had, or had to spare—
Not for me to ask which, when what he took
Had beauties he had to point me out at length
To insure their not being wasted on me.
He liked to have it slender as a whipstock,
70 Free from the least knot, equal to the strain
Of bending like a sword across the knee.
He showed me that the lines of a good helve
Were native to the grain before the knife
Expressed them, and its curves were no false curves
75 Put on it from without. And there its strength lay
For the hard work. He chafed its long white body
From end to end with his rough hand shut round it.
He tried it at the eye-hole in the ax-head.
"Hahn, hahn," he mused, "don't need much taking down."
80 Baptiste knew how to make a short job long
For love of it, and yet not waste time either.

Do you know, what we talked about was knowledge?
Baptiste on his defense about the children
He kept from school, or did his best to keep—
85 Whatever school and children and our doubts
Of laid-on education had to do
With the curves of his ax-helves and his having
Used these unscrupulously to bring me

To see for once the inside of his house.
90   Was I desired in friendship, partly as someone
To leave it to, whether the right to hold
Such doubts of education should depend
Upon the education of those who held them?

But now he brushed the shavings from his knee
95   And stood the ax there on its horse's hoof,
Erect, but not without its waves, as when
The snake stood up for evil in the Garden,—
Top-heavy with a heaviness his short,
Thick hand made light of, steel-blue chin drawn down
100 And in a little—a French touch in that.
Baptiste drew back and squinted at it, pleased:
"See how she's cock her head!"

THE GRINDSTONE

Having a wheel and four legs of its own
Has never availed the cumbersome grindstone
To get it anywhere that I can see.
These hands have helped it go, and even race;
5   Not all the motion, though, they ever lent,
Not all the miles it may have thought it went,
Have got it one step from the starting place.
It stands beside the same old apple tree.
The shadow of the apple tree is thin
10   Upon it now, its feet are fast in snow.
All other farm machinery's gone in,
And some of it on no more legs and wheel
Than the grindstone can boast to stand or go.
(I'm thinking chiefly of the wheelbarrow.)
15   For months it hasn't known the taste of steel,
Washed down with rusty water in a tin.
But standing outdoors hungry, in the cold,
Except in towns at night, is not a sin.
And, anyway, its standing in the yard
20   Under a ruinous live apple tree
Has nothing any more to do with me.
Except that I remember how of old
One summer day, all day I drove it hard,
And someone mounted on it rode it hard,
25   And he and I between us ground a blade.

I gave it the preliminary spin,
And poured on water (tears it might have been);
And when it almost gaily jumped and flowed,
A Father-Time-like man got on and rode,
30   Armed with a scythe and spectacles that glowed.
He turned on will-power to increase the load

And slow me down—and I abruptly slowed,
Like coming to a sudden railroad station.
I changed from hand to hand in desperation.
35 I wondered what machine of ages gone
This represented an improvement on.
For all I knew it may have sharpened spears
And arrowheads itself. Much use for years
Had gradually worn it an oblate
40 Spheroid that kicked and struggled in its gait,
Appearing to return me hate for hate;
(But I forgive it now as easily
As any other boyhood enemy
Whose pride has failed to get him anywhere).
45 I wondered who it was the man thought ground—
The one who held the wheel back or the one
Who gave his life to keep it going round?
I wondered if he really thought it fair
For him to have to say when we were done.
50 Such were the bitter thoughts to which I turned.

Not for myself was I so much concerned.
Oh no!—although, of course, I could have found
A better way to pass the afternoon
Than grinding discord out of a grindstone,
55 And beating insects at their gritty tune.
Nor was I for the man so much concerned.
Once when the grindstone almost jumped its bearing
It looked as if he might be badly thrown
And wounded on his blade. So far from caring,
60 I laughed inside, and only cranked the faster,
(It ran as if it wasn't greased but glued);
I'd welcome any moderate disaster

That might be calculated to postpone
What evidently nothing could conclude.
65 The thing that made me more and more afraid
Was that we'd ground it sharp and hadn't known,
And now were only wasting precious blade.
And when he raised it dripping once and tried
The creepy edge of it with wary touch,
70 And viewed it over his glasses funny-eyed,
Only disinterestedly to decide
It needed a turn more, I could have cried
Wasn't there danger of a turn too much?
Mightn't we make it worse instead of better?
75 I was for leaving something to the whetter.
What if it wasn't all it should be? I'd
Be satisfied if he'd be satisfied.

PAUL'S WIFE

To drive Paul out of any lumber camp
All that was needed was to say to him,
"How is the wife, Paul?"—and he'd disappear.
Some said it was because he had no wife,
And hated to be twitted on the subject;
Others because he'd come within a day
Or so of having one, and then been jilted;
Others because he'd had one once, a good one,
Who'd run away with someone else and left him;
And others still because he had one now
He only had to be reminded of,—
He was all duty to her in a minute:
He had to run right off to look her up,
As if to say, "That's so, how *is* my wife?
I hope she isn't getting into mischief."
No one was anxious to get rid of Paul.
He'd been the hero of the mountain camps
Ever since, just to show them, he had slipped
The bark of a whole tamarack off whole,
As clean as boys do off a willow twig
To make a willow whistle on a Sunday
In April by subsiding meadow brooks.
They seemed to ask him just to see him go,
"How is the wife, Paul?" and he always went.
He never stopped to murder anyone
Who asked the question. He just disappeared—
Nobody knew in what direction,
Although it wasn't usually long
Before they heard of him in some new camp,
The same Paul at the same old feats of logging.
The question everywhere was why should Paul
Object to being asked a civil question—

A man you could say almost anything to
Short of a fighting word. You have the answers.
35 And there was one more not so fair to Paul:
That Paul had married a wife not his equal.
Paul was ashamed of her. To match a hero,
She would have had to be a heroine;
Instead of which she was some half-breed squaw.
40 But if the story Murphy told was true,
She wasn't any one to be ashamed of.

You know Paul could do wonders. Everyone's
Heard how he thrashed the horses on a load
That wouldn't budge until they simply stretched
45 Their rawhide harness from the load to camp.
Paul told the boss the load would be all right,
"The sun will bring your load in"—and it did—
By shrinking the rawhide to natural length.
That's what is called a stretcher. But I guess
50 The one about his jumping so's to land
With both his feet at once against the ceiling,
And then land safely right side up again,
Back on the floor, is fact or pretty near fact.
Well, this is such a yarn. Paul sawed his wife
55 Out of a white-pine log. Murphy was there,
And, as you might say, saw the lady born.
Paul worked at anything in lumbering.
He'd been hard at it taking boards away
For—I forget—the last ambitious sawyer
60 To want to find out if he couldn't pile
The lumber on Paul till Paul begged for mercy.
They'd sliced the first slab off a big butt log,
And the sawyer had slammed the carriage back

To slam end on again against the saw teeth.
65 To judge them by the way they caught themselves
When they saw what had happened to the log,
They must have had a guilty expectation
Something was going to go with their slambanging.
Something had left a long black streak of grease
70 On the new wood the whole length of the log
Except, perhaps, a foot at either end.
But when Paul put his finger in the grease,
It wasn't grease at all, but a long slot.
The log was hollow. They were sawing pine.
75 "First time I ever saw a hollow pine.
That comes of having Paul around the place.
Take it to hell for me," the sawyer said.
Everyone had to have a look at it,
And tell Paul what he ought to do about it.
80 (They treated it as his.) "You take a jack-knife,
And spread the opening, and you've got a dug-out
All dug to go a-fishing in." To Paul
The hollow looked too sound and clean and empty
Ever to have housed birds or beasts or bees.
85 There was no entrance for them to get in by.
It looked to him like some new kind of hollow
He thought he'd *better* take his jack-knife to.
So after work that evening he came back
And let enough light into it by cutting
90 To see if it was empty. He made out in there
A slender length of pith, or was it pith?
It might have been the skin a snake had cast
And left stood up on end inside the tree
The hundred years the tree must have been growing
95 More cutting and he had this in both hands,

And looking from it to the pond nearby,
Paul wondered how it would respond to water.
Not a breeze stirred, but just the breath of air
He made in walking slowly to the beach
100   Blew it once off his hands and almost broke it.
He laid it at the edge, where it could drink.
At the first drink it rustled and grew limp.
At the next drink it grew invisible.
Paul dragged the shallows for it with his fingers,
105   And thought it must have melted. It was gone.
And then beyond the open water, dim with midges,
Where the log drive lay pressed against the boom,
It slowly rose a person, rose a girl,
Her wet hair heavy on her like a helmet,
110   Who, leaning on a log, looked back at Paul.
And that made Paul in turn look back
To see if it was anyone behind him
That she was looking at instead of him.
(Murphy had been there watching all the time,
115   But from a shed where neither of them could see him.)
There was a moment of suspense in birth
When the girl seemed too water-logged to live,
Before she caught her first breath with a gasp
And laughed. Then she climbed slowly to her feet,
120   And walked off talking to herself or Paul,
Across the logs like backs of alligators,
Paul taking after her around the pond.

Next evening Murphy and some other fellows
Got drunk, and tracked the pair up Catamount,
125   From the bare top of which there is a view
To other hills across a kettle valley.

And there, well after dark, let Murphy tell it,
They saw Paul and his creature keeping house.
It was the only glimpse that anyone
130 Has had of Paul and her since Murphy saw them
Falling in love across the twilight mill-pond.
More than a mile across the wilderness
They sat together halfway up a cliff
In a small niche let into it, the girl
135 Brightly, as if a star played on the place,
Paul darkly, like her shadow. All the light
Was from the girl herself, though, not a star,
As was apparent from what happened next.
All those great ruffians put their throats together,
140 And let out a loud yell, and threw a bottle,
As a brute tribute of respect to beauty.
Of course the bottle fell short by a mile,
But the shout reached the girl and put her light out.
She went out like a firefly, and that was all.

145 So there were witnesses that Paul was married,
And not to anyone to be ashamed of.
Everyone had been wrong in judging Paul.
Murphy told me Paul put on all those airs
About his wife to keep her to himself.
150 Paul was what's called a terrible possessor.
Owning a wife with him meant owning her.
She wasn't anybody else's business,
Either to praise her, or so much as name her
And he'd thank people not to think of her.
155 Murphy's idea was that a man like Paul
Wouldn't be spoken to about a wife
In any way the world knew how to speak in.

WILD GRAPES[39]

What tree may not the fig be gathered from?
The grape may not be gathered from the birch?
It's all you know the grape, or know the birch.[40]
As a girl gathered from the birch myself
5 Equally with my weight in grapes, one autumn,
I ought to know what tree the grape is fruit of.
I was born, I suppose, like anyone,
And grew to be a little boyish girl
My brother could not always leave at home.
10 But that beginning was wiped out in fear
The day I swung suspended with the grapes,
And was come after like Eurydice[41]
And brought down safely from the upper regions;
And the life I live now's an extra life
15 I can waste as I please on whom I please.
So if you see me celebrate two birthdays,
And give myself out of two different ages,
One of them five years younger than I look—

One day my brother led me to a glade
20 Where a white birch he knew of stood alone,
Wearing a thin headdress of pointed leaves,
And heavy on her heavy hair behind,
Against her neck, an ornament of grapes.
Grapes, I knew grapes from having seen them last year.
25 One bunch of them, and there began to be
Bunches all round me growing in white birches,
The way they grew round Leif the Lucky's German;[42]
Mostly as much beyond my lifted hands, though,
As the moon used to seem when I was younger,
30 And only freely to be had for climbing.
My brother did the climbing; and at first

Threw me down grapes to miss and scatter
And have to hunt for in sweet fern and hardhack;
Which gave him some time to himself to eat,
35 But not so much, perhaps, as a boy needed.
So then, to make me wholly self-supporting,
He climbed still higher and bent the tree to earth
And put it in my hands to pick my own grapes.
"Here, take a tree-top, I'll get down another.
40 Hold on with all your might when I let go."
I said I had the tree. It wasn't true.
The opposite was true. The tree had me.
The minute it was left with me alone,
It caught me up as if I were the fish
45 And it the fishpole. So I was translated
To loud cries from my brother of "Let go!
Don't you know anything, you girl? Let go!"
But I, with something of the baby grip
Acquired ancestrally in just such trees
50 When wilder mothers than our wildest now
Hung babies out on branches by the hands
To dry or wash or tan, I don't know which
(You'll have to ask an evolutionist)—
I held on uncomplainingly for life.
55 My brother tried to make me laugh to help me.
"What are you doing up there in those grapes?
Don't be afraid. A few of them won't hurt you.
I mean, they won't pick you if you don't them."
Much danger of my picking anything!
60 By that time I was pretty well reduced
To a philosophy of hang-and-let-hang.
"Now you know how it feels," my brother said,
"To be a bunch of fox grapes, as they call them,

That when it thinks it has escaped the fox
65 By growing where it shouldn't—on a birch,
Where a fox wouldn't think to look for it—
And if he looked and found it, couldn't reach it—
Just then come you and I to gather it.
Only you have the advantage of the grapes
70 In one way: you have one more stem to cling by,
And promise more resistance to the picker."

One by one I lost off my hat and shoes,
And still I clung. I let my head fall back,
And shut my eyes against the sun, my ears
75 Against my brother's nonsense; "Drop," he said,
"I'll catch you in my arms. It isn't far."
(Stated in lengths of him it might not be.)
"Drop or I'll shake the tree and shake you down."
Grim silence on my part as I sank lower,
80 My small wrists stretching till they showed the banjo strings.
"Why, if she isn't serious about it!
Hold tight awhile till I think what to do.
I'll bend the tree down and let you down by it."
I don't know much about the letting down;
85 But once I felt ground with my stocking feet
And the world came revolving back to me,
I know I looked long at my curled-up fingers,
Before I straightened them and brushed the bark off.
My brother said: "Don't you weigh anything?
90 Try to weigh something next time, so you won't
Be run off with by birch trees into space."

It wasn't my not weighing anything
So much as my not knowing anything—

My brother had been nearer right before.
95 I had not taken the first step in knowledge;
I had not learned to let go with the hands,
As still I have not learned to with the heart,
And have no wish to with the heart—nor need,
That I can see. The mind—is not the heart.
100 I may yet live, as I know others live,
To wish in vain to let go with the mind—
Of cares, at night, to sleep; but nothing tells me
That I need learn to let go with the heart.

Place for a Third

Nothing to say to all those marriages!
She had made three herself to three of his.
The score was even for them, three to three.
But come to die she found she cared so much:
5   She thought of children in a burial row;
Three children in a burial row were sad.
One man's three women in a burial row
Somehow made her impatient with the man.
And so she said to Laban, "You have done
10 A good deal right; don't do the last thing wrong.
Don't make me lie with those two other women."

Laban said, No, he would not make her lie
With anyone but that she had a mind to,
If that was how she felt, of course, he said.
15 She went her way. But Laban having caught
This glimpse of lingering person in Eliza,
And anxious to make all he could of it
With something he remembered in himself,
Tried to think how he could exceed his promise,
20 And give good measure to the dead, though thankless.
If that was how she felt, he kept repeating.
His first thought under pressure was a grave
In a new boughten grave plot by herself,
Under he didn't care how great a stone:
25 He'd sell a yoke of steers to pay for it.
And weren't there special cemetery flowers,
That, once grief sets to growing, grief may rest:
The flowers will go on with grief awhile,
And no one seem neglecting or neglected?
30 A prudent grief will not despise such aids.
He thought of evergreen and everlasting.

And then he had a thought worth many of these.
Somewhere must be the grave of the young boy
Who married her for playmate more than helpmate,
And sometimes laughed at what it was between them.
How would she like to sleep her last with him?
Where was his grave? Did Laban know his name?

He found the grave a town or two away,
The headstone cut with *John, Beloved Husband,*
Beside it room reserved, the say a sister's,
A never-married sister's of that husband,
Whether Eliza would be welcome there.
The dead was bound to silence: ask the sister.
So Laban saw the sister, and, saying nothing
Of where Eliza wanted *not* to lie,
And who had thought to lay her with her first love,
Begged simply for the grave. The sister's face
Fell all in wrinkles of responsibility.
She wanted to do right. She'd have to think.
Laban was old and poor, yet seemed to care;
And she was old and poor—but she cared, too.
They sat. She cast one dull, old look at him,
Then turned him out to go on other errands
She said he might attend to in the village,
While she made up her mind how much she cared—
And how much Laban cared—and why he cared,
(She made shrewd eyes to see where he came in.)

She'd looked Eliza up her second time,
A widow at her second husband's grave,
And offered her a home to rest awhile
Before she went the poor man's widow's way,

Housekeeping for the next man out of wedlock.
She and Eliza had been friends through all.
Who was she to judge marriage in a world
65 Whose Bible's so confused up in marriage counsel?
The sister had not come across this Laban;
A decent product of life's ironing-out;
She must not keep him waiting. Time would press
Between the death day and the funeral day.
70 So when she saw him coming in the street
She hurried her decision to be ready
To meet him with his answer at the door.
Laban had known about what it would be
From the way she had set her poor old mouth,
75 To do, as she had put it, what was right.

She gave it through the screen door closed between them:
"No, not with John. There wouldn't be no sense.
Eliza's had too many other men."

Laban was forced to fall back on his plan
80 To buy Eliza a plot to lie alone in:
Which gives him for himself a choice of lots
When his time comes to die and settle down.

Two Witches

I
THE WITCH OF COÖS[43]

I stayed the night for shelter at a farm
Behind the mountain, with a mother and son,
Two old-believers. They did all the talking.

MOTHER. Folks think a witch who has familiar spirits
5   She *could* call up to pass a winter evening,
But *won't,* should be burned at the stake or something.
Summoning spirits isn't "Button, button,
Who's got the button," you're to understand.

SON. Mother can make a common table rear
10 And kick with two legs like an army mule.

MOTHER. And when I've done it, what good have I done?
Rather than tip a table for you, let me
Tell you what Ralle the Sioux Control[44] once told me.
He said the dead had souls, but when I asked him
15 How that could be—I thought the dead were souls,
He broke my trance. Don't that make you suspicious
That there's something the dead are keeping back?
Yes, there's something the dead are keeping back.

SON. You wouldn't want to tell him what we have
Up attic, mother?

20 MOTHER. Bones—a skeleton.

SON. But the headboard of mother's bed is pushed
Against the attic door: the door is nailed.

It's harmless. Mother hears it in the night
Halting perplexed behind the barrier
25 Of door and headboard. Where it wants to get
Is back into the cellar where it came from.

MOTHER. We'll never let them, will we, son? We'll never!

SON. It left the cellar forty years ago
And carried itself like a pile of dishes
30 Up one flight from the cellar to the kitchen,
Another from the kitchen to the bedroom,
Another from the bedroom to the attic,
Right past both father and mother, and neither stopped it.
Father had gone upstairs; mother was downstairs.
35 I was a baby: I don't know where I was.

MOTHER. The only fault my husband found with me—
I went to sleep before I went to bed,
Especially in winter when the bed
Might just as well be ice and the clothes snow.
40 The night the bones came up the cellar-stairs
Toffile had gone to bed alone and left me,
But left an open door to cool the room off
So as to sort of turn me out of it.
I was just coming to myself enough
45 To wonder where the cold was coming from,
When I heard Toffile upstairs in the bedroom
And thought I heard him downstairs in the cellar.
The board we had laid down to walk dry-shod on
When there was water in the cellar in spring
50 Struck the hard cellar bottom. And then someone

Began the stairs, two footsteps for each step,
The way a man with one leg and a crutch,
Or little child, comes up. It wasn't Toffile:
It wasn't anyone who could be there.
55 The bulkhead double-doors were double-locked
And swollen tight and buried under snow.
The cellar windows were banked up with sawdust
And swollen tight and buried under snow.
It was the bones. I knew them—and good reason.
60 My first impulse was to get to the knob
And hold the door. But the bones didn't try
The door; they halted helpless on the landing,
Waiting for things to happen in their favor.
The faintest restless rustling ran all through them.
65 I never could have done the thing I did
If the wish hadn't been too strong in me
To see how they were mounted for this walk.
I had a vision of them put together
Not like a man, but like a chandelier.
70 So suddenly I flung the door wide on him.
A moment he stood balancing with emotion,
And all but lost himself. (A tongue of fire
Flashed out and licked along his upper teeth.
Smoke rolled inside the sockets of his eyes.)
75 Then he came at me with one hand outstretched,
The way he did in life once; but this time
I struck the hand off brittle on the floor,
And fell back from him on the floor myself.
The finger-pieces slid in all directions.
80 (Where did I see one of those pieces lately?
Hand me my button-box—it must be there.)
I sat up on the floor and shouted, "Toffile,

It's coming up to you." It had its choice
Of the door to the cellar or the hall.
85 It took the hall door for the novelty,
And set off briskly for so slow a thing,
Still going every which way in the joints, though,
So that it looked like lightning or a scribble,
From the slap I had just now given its hand.
90 I listened till it almost climbed the stairs
From the hall to the only finished bedroom,
Before I got up to do anything;
Then ran and shouted, "Shut the bedroom door,
Toffile, for my sake!" "Company?" he said,
95 "Don't make me get up; I'm too warm in bed."
So lying forward weakly on the handrail
I pushed myself upstairs, and in the light
(The kitchen had been dark) I had to own
I could see nothing. "Toffile, I don't see it.
100 It's with us in the room, though. It's the bones."
"What bones?" "The cellar bones—out of the grave."
That made him throw his bare legs out of bed
And sit up by me and take hold of me.
I wanted to put out the light and see
105 If I could see it, or else mow the room,
With our arms at the level of our knees,
And bring the chalk-pile down. "I'll tell you what—
It's looking for another door to try.
The uncommonly deep snow has made him think
110 Of his old song, *The Wild Colonial Boy,*[45]
He always used to sing along the tote road.
He's after an open door to get outdoors.
Let's trap him with an open door up attic."
Toffile agreed to that, and sure enough,

115   Almost the moment he was given an opening,
The steps began to climb the attic stairs.
I heard them. Toffile didn't seem to hear them.
"Quick!" I slammed to the door and held the knob.
"Toffile, get nails." I made him nail the door shut
120 And push the headboard of the bed against it.
Then we asked was there anything
Up attic that we'd ever want again.
The attic was less to us than the cellar.
If the bones liked the attic, let them like it.
125 Let them *stay* in the attic. When they sometimes
Come down the stairs at night and stand perplexed
Behind the door and headboard of the bed,
Brushing their chalky skull with chalky fingers,
With sounds like the dry rattling of a shutter,
130 That's what I sit up in the dark to say—
To no one any more since Toffile died.
Let them stay in the attic since they went there.
I promised Toffile to be cruel to them
For helping them be cruel once to him.

135 SON. We think they had a grave down in the cellar.

MOTHER. We know they had a grave down in the cellar.

SON. We never could find out whose bones they were.

MOTHER. Yes, we could too, son. Tell the truth for once.
They were a man's his father killed for me.
140 I mean a man he killed instead of me.
The least I could do was help dig their grave.
We were about it one night in the cellar.

Son knows the story: but 'twas not for him
To tell the truth, suppose the time had come.
145　Son looks surprised to see me end a lie
We'd kept up all these years between ourselves
So as to have it ready for outsiders.
But tonight I don't care enough to lie—
I don't remember why I ever cared.
150　Toffile, if he were here, I don't believe
Could tell you why he ever cared himself. . . .

She hadn't found the finger-bone she wanted
Among the buttons poured out in her lap.
I verified the name next morning: Toffile.
155　The rural letter box said Toffile Lajway.

II

THE PAUPER WITCH OF GRAFTON[46]

Now that they've got it settled whose I be,
I'm going to tell them something they won't like:
They've got it settled wrong, and I can prove it.
Flattered I must be to have two towns fighting
5　To make a present of me to each other.
They don't dispose me, either one of them,
To spare them any trouble. Double trouble's
Always the witch's motto anyway.
I'll double theirs for both of them—you watch me.
10　They'll find they've got the whole thing to do over,
That is, if facts is what they want to go by.
They set a lot (now don't they?) by a record
Of Arthur Amy's having once been up
For Hog Reeve in March Meeting here in Warren.

15   I could have told them any time this twelvemonth
     The Arthur Amy I was married to
     Couldn't have been the one they say was up
     In Warren at March Meeting for the reason
     He wa'n't but fifteen at the time they say.
20   The Arthur Amy I was married to
     Voted the only times he ever voted,
     Which wasn't many, in the town of Wentworth.
     One of the times was when 'twas in the warrant
     To see if the town wanted to take over
25   The tote road to our clearing where we lived.
     I'll tell you who'd remember—Heman Lapish.
     Their Arthur Amy was the father of mine.
     So now they've dragged it through the law courts once
     I guess they'd better drag it through again.
30   Wentworth and Warren's both good towns to live in,
     Only I happen to prefer to live
     In Wentworth from now on; and when all's said,
     Right's right, and the temptation to do right
     When I can hurt someone by doing it
35   Has always been too much for me, it has.
     I know of some folks that'd be set up
     At having in their town a noted witch:
     But most would have to think of the expense
     That even I would be. They ought to know
40   That as a witch I'd often milk a bat
     And that'd be enough to last for days.
     It'd make my position stronger, think,
     If I was to consent to give some sign
     To make it surer that I was a witch?
45   It wa'n't no sign, I s'pose, when Mallice Huse
     Said that I took him out in his old age

And rode all over everything on him
Until I'd had him worn to skin and bones,
And if I'd left him hitched unblanketed
50   In front of one Town Hall, I'd left him hitched
In front of every one in Grafton County.
Some cried shame on me not to blanket him,
The poor old man. It would have been all right
If someone hadn't said to gnaw the posts
55   He stood beside and leave his trade mark on them,
So they could recognize them. Not a post
That they could hear tell of was scarified.
They made him keep on gnawing till he whined.
Then that same smarty someone said to look—
60   He'd bet Huse was a cribber and had gnawed
The crib he slept in—and as sure's you're born
They found he'd gnawed the four posts of his bed,
All four of them to splinters. What did that prove?
Not that he hadn't gnawed the hitching posts
65   He said he had besides. Because a horse
Gnaws in the stable ain't no proof to me
He don't gnaw trees and posts and fences too.
But everybody took it for a proof.
I was a strapping girl of twenty then.
70   The smarty someone who spoiled everything
Was Arthur Amy. You know who he was.
That was the way he started courting me.
He never said much after we were married,
But I mistrusted he was none too proud
75   Of having interfered in the Huse business.
I guess he found he got more out of me
By having me a witch. Or something happened
To turn him round. He got to saying things

To undo what he'd done and make it right,
Like, "No, she ain't come back from kiting yet.
Last night was one of her nights out. She's kiting.
She thinks when the wind makes a night of it
She might as well herself." But he liked best
To let on he was plagued to death with me:
If anyone had seen me coming home
Over the ridgepole, 'stride of a broomstick,
As often as he had in the tail of the night,
He guessed they'd know what he had to put up with.
Well, I showed Arthur Amy signs enough
Off from the house as far as we could keep
And from barn smells you can't wash out of plowed ground
With all the rain and snow of seven years;
And I don't mean just skulls of Rogers' Rangers[47]
On Moosilauke, but woman signs to man,
Only bewitched so I would last him longer.
Up where the trees grow short, the mosses tall,
I made him gather me wet snow berries
On slippery rocks beside a waterfall.
I made him do it for me in the dark.
And he liked everything I made him do.
I hope if he is where he sees me now
He's so far off he can't see what I've come to.
You *can* come down from everything to nothing.
All is, if I'd a-known when I was young
And full of it, that this would be the end,
It doesn't seem as if I'd had the courage
To make so free and kick up in folks' faces.
I might have, but it doesn't seem as if.

Fire and Ice

Some say the world will end in fire,
Some say in ice.
From what I've tasted of desire
I hold with those who favor fire.
5   But if it had to perish twice,
I think I know enough of hate
To say that for destruction ice
Is also great
And would suffice.

DUST OF SNOW

The way a crow
Shook down on me
The dust of snow
From a hemlock tree

5   Has given my heart
A change of mood
And saved some part
Of a day I had rued.

To E. T.

I slumbered with your poems[48] on my breast
Spread open as I dropped them half-read through
Like dove wings on a figure on a tomb
To see, if in a dream they brought of you,

5 I might not have the chance I missed in life
Through some delay, and call you to your face
First soldier, and then poet, and then both,
Who died a soldier-poet of your race.

I meant, you meant, that nothing should remain
10 Unsaid between us, brother, and this remained—
And one thing more that was not then to say:
The Victory for what it lost and gained.

You went to meet the shell's embrace of fire
On Vimy Ridge;[49] and when you fell that day
15 The war seemed over more for you than me,
But now for me than you—the other way.

How over, though, for even me who knew
The foe thrust back unsafe beyond the Rhine,
If I was not to speak of it to you
20 And see you pleased once more with words of mine?

THE AIM WAS SONG

Before man came to blow it right
    The wind once blew itself untaught,
And did its loudest day and night
    In any rough place where it caught.

5 Man came to tell it what was wrong:
    It hadn't found the place to blow;
It blew too hard—the aim was song.
    And listen—how it ought to go!

He took a little in his mouth,
10   And held it long enough for north
To be converted into south,
    And then by measure blew it forth.

By measure. It was word and note,
    The wind the wind had meant to be—
15 A little through the lips and throat.
    The aim was song—the wind could see.

For Once, Then, Something

Others taunt me with having knelt at well-curbs
Always wrong to the light, so never seeing
Deeper down in the well than where the water
Gives me back in a shining surface picture
5   Me myself in the summer heaven godlike
Looking out of a wreath of fern and cloud puffs.
Once, when trying with chin against a well-curb,
I discerned, as I thought, beyond the picture,
Through the picture, a something white, uncertain,
10 Something more of the depths—and then I lost it.
Water came to rebuke the too clear water.
One drop fell from a fern, and lo, a ripple
Shook whatever it was lay there at bottom,
Blurred it, blotted it out. What was that whiteness?
15 Truth? A pebble of quartz?[50] For once, then, something.

BLUE-BUTTERFLY DAY

It is blue-butterfly day here in spring,
And with these sky-flakes down in flurry on flurry
There is more unmixed color on the wing
Than flowers will show for days unless they hurry.

₅ But these are flowers that fly and all but sing:
And now from having ridden out desire
They lie closed over in the wind and cling
Where wheels have freshly sliced the April mire.

THE ONSET

Always the same, when on a fated night
At last the gathered snow lets down as white
As may be in dark woods, and with a song
It shall not make again all winter long
5   Of hissing on the yet uncovered ground,
I almost stumble looking up and round,
As one who overtaken by the end
Gives up his errand, and lets death descend
Upon him where he is, with nothing done
10 To evil, no important triumph won,
More than if life had never been begun.

Yet all the precedent is on my side:
I know that winter death has never tried
The earth but it has failed: the snow may heap
15 In long storms an undrifted four feet deep
As measured against maple, birch, and oak,
It cannot check the peeper's silver croak;
And I shall see the snow all go down hill
In water of a slender April rill
20 That flashes tail through last year's withered brake
And dead weeds, like a disappearing snake.
Nothing will be left white but here a birch,
And there a clump of houses with a church.

Good-by and Keep Cold

This saying good-by on the edge of the dark
And cold to an orchard so young in the bark
Reminds me of all that can happen to harm
An orchard away at the end of the farm
5   All winter, cut off by a hill from the house.
I don't want it girdled by rabbit and mouse,
I don't want it dreamily nibbled for browse
By deer, and I don't want it budded by grouse.
(If certain it wouldn't be idle to call
10   I'd summon grouse, rabbit, and deer to the wall
And warn them away with a stick for a gun.)
I don't want it stirred by the heat of the sun.
(We made it secure against being, I hope,
By setting it out on a northerly slope.)
15   No orchard's the worse for the wintriest storm;
But one thing about it, it mustn't get warm.
"How often already you've had to be told,
Keep cold, young orchard. Good-by and keep cold.
Dread fifty above more than fifty below."
20   I have to be gone for a season or so.
My business awhile is with different trees,
Less carefully nourished, less fruitful than these,
And such as is done to their wood with an ax—
Maples and birches and tamaracks.
25   I wish I could promise to lie in the night
And think of an orchard's arboreal plight
When slowly (and nobody comes with a light)
Its heart sinks lower under the sod.
But something has to be left to God.

NOT TO KEEP

They sent him back to her. The letter came
Saying . . . And she could have him. And before
She could be sure there was no hidden ill
Under the formal writing, he was in her sight,
5   Living. They gave him back to her alive—
How else? They are not known to send the dead—
And not disfigured visibly. His face?
His hands? She had to look, to ask,
"What was it, dear?" And she had given all
10 And still she had all—*they* had—they the lucky!
Wasn't she glad now? Everything seemed won,
And all the rest for them permissible ease.
She had to ask, "What was it, dear?"

                         "Enough,
Yet not enough. A bullet through and through,
15 High in the breast. Nothing but what good care
And medicine and rest, and you a week,
Can cure me of to go again." The same
Grim giving to do over for them both.
She dared no more than ask him with her eyes
20 How was it with him for a second trial.
And with his eyes he asked her not to ask.
They had given him back to her, but not to keep.

A Brook in the City

The farmhouse lingers, though averse to square
With the new city street it has to wear
A number in. But what about the brook
That held the house as in an elbow-crook?
5 I ask as one who knew the brook, its strength
And impulse, having dipped a finger length
And made it leap my knuckle, having tossed
A flower to try its currents where they crossed.
The meadow grass could be cemented down
10 From growing under pavements of a town;
The apple trees be sent to hearth-stone flame.
Is water wood to serve a brook the same?
How else dispose of an immortal force
No longer needed? Staunch it at its source
15 With cinder loads dumped down? The brook was thrown
Deep in a sewer dungeon under stone
In fetid darkness still to live and run—
And all for nothing it had ever done
Except forget to go in fear perhaps.
20 No one would know except for ancient maps
That such a brook ran water. But I wonder
If from its being kept forever under
These thoughts may not have risen that so keep
This new-built city from both work and sleep.

Evening in a Sugar Orchard

From where I lingered in a lull of March
Outside the sugar-house one night for choice,
I called the fireman in a quiet voice
And bade him leave the pan and stoke the arch:
5   "O fireman, give the fire another stoke,
And send more sparks up chimney with the smoke."
I thought a few might tangle, as they did,
Among bare maple boughs, and in the rare
Hill atmosphere not cease to glow,
10 And so be added to the moon up there.
The moon, though slight, was moon enough to show
On every tree a bucket with a lid,
And on black ground one bear-skin rug of snow.
The sparks made no attempt to be the moon.
15 They were content to figure in the trees
As Leo, Orion, and the Pleiades.
And that was what the boughs were full of soon.

The Valley's Singing Day

The sound of the closing outside door was all.
You made no sound in the grass with your footfall,
As far as you went from the door, which was not far;
But you had awakened under the morning star
5   The first song-bird that awakened all the rest.
He could have slept but a moment more at best.
Already determined dawn began to lay
In place across a cloud the slender ray
For prying beneath and forcing the lids of sight,
10   And loosing the pent-up music of over-night.
But dawn was not to begin their "pearly-pearly"
(By which they mean the rain is pearls so early,
Before it changes to diamonds in the sun),
Neither was song that day to be self-begun.
15   You had begun it, and if there needed proof—
I was asleep still under the dripping roof,
My window curtain hung over the sill to wet;
But I should awake to confirm your story yet;
I should be willing to say and help you say
20   That once you had opened the valley's singing day.

MISGIVING

All crying, "We will go with you, O Wind!"
The foliage follow him, leaf and stem;
But a sleep oppresses them as they go,
And they end by bidding him stay with them.

5   Since ever they flung abroad in spring
The leaves have promised themselves this flight,
Who now would fain seek sheltering wall,
Or thicket, or hollow place for the night.

And now they answer the summoning blast
10 With an ever vaguer and vaguer stir,
Or at utmost a little reluctant whirl
That drops them no further than where they were.

I only hope that when I am free,
As they are free, to go in quest
15 Of the knowledge beyond the bounds of life
It may not seem better to *me* to rest.

A Hillside Thaw

To think to know the country and not know
The hillside on the day the sun lets go
Ten million silver lizards out of snow!
As often as I've seen it done before
5   I can't pretend to tell the way it's done.
It looks as if some magic of the sun
Lifted the rug that bred them on the floor
And the light breaking on them made them run.
But if I thought to stop the wet stampede,
10 And caught one silver lizard by the tail,
And put my foot on one without avail,
And threw myself wet-elbowed and wet-kneed
In front of twenty others' wriggling speed,—
In the confusion of them all aglitter,
15 And birds that joined in the excited fun
By doubling and redoubling song and twitter,
I have no doubt I'd end by holding none.

It takes the moon for this. The sun's a wizard
By all I tell; but so's the moon a witch.
20 From the high west she makes a gentle cast
And suddenly, without a jerk or twitch,
She has her spell on every single lizard.
I fancied when I looked at eight o'clock
The swarm still ran and scuttled just as fast.
25 The moon was waiting for her chill effect.
I looked at ten: the swarm was turned to rock
In every lifelike posture of the swarm,
Transfixed on mountain slopes almost erect.
Across each other and side by side they lay.
30 The spell that so could hold them as they were
Was wrought through trees without a breath of storm

To make a leaf, if there had been one, stir.
It was the moon's: she held them until day,
One lizard at the end of every ray.
35   The thought of my attempting such a stay!

PLOWMEN

A plow, I hear men say, to plow the snow.
They cannot mean to plant it, though—
Unless in bitterness to mock
At having cultivated rock.

ON A TREE FALLEN ACROSS THE ROAD

The tree the tempest with a crash of wood
Throws down in front of us is not to bar
Our passage to our journey's end for good,
But just to ask us who we think we are

5   Insisting always on our own way so.
She likes to halt us in our runner tracks,
And make us get down in a foot of snow
Debating what to do without an ax.

And yet she knows obstruction is in vain:
10   We will not be put off the final goal
We have it hidden in us to attain,
Not though we have to seize by either pole

This aimless earth now circling in one place,
And steer it a direction straight through space.

THE LOCKLESS DOOR

It went many years,
But at last came a knock,
And I thought of the door
With no lock to lock.

5   I blew out the light,
I tip-toed the floor,
And raised both hands
In prayer to the door.

But the knock came again
10   My window was wide;
I climbed on the sill
And descended outside.

Back over the sill
I bade a "Come in"
15   To whoever the knock
At the door may have been.

So at a knock
I emptied my cage
To hide in the world
20   And alter with age.

THE NEED OF BEING VERSED IN
COUNTRY THINGS

The house had gone to bring again
To the midnight sky a sunset glow.
Now the chimney was all of the house that stood,
Like a pistil after the petals go.

5 The barn opposed across the way,
That would have joined the house in flame
Had it been the will of the wind, was left
To bear forsaken the place's name.

No more it opened with all one end
10 For teams that came by the stony road
To drum on the floor with scurrying hoofs
And brush the mow with the summer load.

The birds that came to it through the air
At broken windows flew out and in,
15 Their murmur more like the sigh we sigh
From too much dwelling on what has been.

Yet for them the lilac renewed its leaf,
And the aged elm, though touched with fire;
And the dry pump flung up an awkward arm;
20 And the fence post carried a strand of wire.

For them there was really nothing sad.
But though they rejoiced in the nest they kept,
One had to be versed in country things
Not to believe the phoebes wept.

EXPLANATORY NOTES

1. *A BOY'S WILL:* Cf. Henry Wadsworth Longfellow, "My Lost Youth" (1858): "A boy's will is the wind's will,/And the thoughts of youth are long, long thoughts." *A Boy's Will* was first published in 1913 in London by David Nutt with the dedication "To E. M. F." (Elinor Miriam Frost, the poet's wife).

2. *the edge of doom:* Cf. Shakespeare's Sonnet 116 ("Let me not to the marriage of true minds"), lines 11–12: "Love alters not with his brief hours and weeks,/But bears it out even to the edge of doom."

3. *Rose Pogonias:* Small orchids found in the eastern United States and known as snake mouth pogonias because of their open pink flowers like a snake's mouth and spear-shaped leaves.

4. *worn book . . . song: Golden Treasury of the Best Songs and Lyrical Poems in the English Language* (1861; rev. 1897), edited by Francis Turner Palgrave; one of Frost's favorite anthologies.

5. *a bright green snake:* Cf. Samuel Taylor Coleridge's "Christabel" (1816), line 549, where a bard reports his surprise in a dream: "When lo! I saw a bright green snake."

6. *Wide fields of asphodel fore'er:* In Greek myths, those favored of the gods lived on in Elysium, also known as the Plain of Asphodel. The asphodel is a member of the lily family and has a yellow flower. It is often associated with death.

7. *The Demiurge's Laugh:* Demiurge is the name for the Maker or Creator of the world in the Platonic philosophy; later, in Gnostic religion, it was conceived as a being subordinate to the Supreme Being, and sometimes as the author of evil.

8. *NORTH OF BOSTON:* First published in 1914 with the dedication "To E. M. F. THIS BOOK OF PEOPLE" and "The Pasture" as a prologue. E. M. F. is Elinor Miriam Frost.

9. *Mending Wall:* The title poem of his fourth book, *New Hampshire*, refers to Napoleon Guay (pronounced "Gay"), a French-Canadian farmer who inspired "The Ax-Helve" and "Mending Wall."

10. *Hor:* Numbers 20:23–24—"And the Lord spake unto Moses and Aaron in mount Hor, by the coast of the land of Edom saying,/ Aaron shall be gathered unto his people: for he shall not enter into the land which I have given unto the children of Israel, because ye rebelled against my word at the water of Meribah."

11. *Lunenburg:* A town in northern Vermont.

12. *Garrison:* William Lloyd Garrison (1805–79), American journalist and abolitionist.

13. *Whittier:* James Greenleaf Whittier (1807–72), American poet.

14. *the principle . . . Welshman got it planted:* In the Declaration of Independence (adopted July 4, 1776), Jefferson wrote, "We hold these truths to be self-evident, that all men are created equal." In his *Autobiography*, Jefferson wrote that his father's ancestors were thought to have come to America from Wales.

15. *Creed . . . Hades:* The Apostle's Creed, where "hell" was sometimes translated "Hades."

16. *chewink:* Finch.

17. *A Servant to Servants:* Genesis 9:25—the curse of Ham for seeing Noah naked, "a servant of servants shall he be unto his brethren."

18. *Bow:* Village in southeast New Hampshire.

19. *"You riddle . . . Viola:* In Shakespeare, *Twelfth Night*, 1.5.298–99, Viola, disguised as a page, responds to a question about her parentage: "Above my fortunes, yet my state is well: I am a gentleman."

20. *Chicamoztoc:* Myth of the pre-Columbian Aztec Indians of Mexico.

21. *Nausicaa:* In Homer's *Odyssey*, book 6, the Phaeacian princess remains unafraid encountering the naked, shipwrecked Odysseus. She guides him to her father, who eventually returns him to Ithaca.

22. *Lagshang:* Large Asiatic breed of poultry.

23. *Crystal Palace, London:* An immense building of glass built in Hyde Park, London, to house the Great Exhibition of 1851; in 1854, it was moved to Sydenham, south of London, where it was used for public exhibits of the achievements of Victorian England, including livestock and poultry shows. It burned down in 1936.

24. *blessed feet?:* Cf. Shakespeare, I *Henry IV*, 1.1.24–26—". . . holy fields/Over whose acres walked those blessed feet/Which fourteen hundred years ago were nailed/For our advantage on the bitter cross."

25. *Burroughs . . . reginæ:* John Burroughs (1837–1921), American naturalist and author; *Cyprepedium reginæ* means "Queen's orchid."

26. *Good Hours:* Not in the first English edition of *North of Boston* (1914); Frost added the poem in the American edition (1915), where it is set at the end in italics.

27. *MOUNTAIN INTERVAL:* An interval, or intervale, is a New England term for low-lying land, especially along a watercourse. *Mountain Interval* was published in 1916 in New York by Henry Holt.

28. *the Hyla breed:* A breed of small tree frogs, called spring peepers, which hibernate underground in winter. See also Charles Darwin's discussion of Hyla frogs in *The Voyage of the Beagle,* chapter 2, "Rio De Janeiro." Also significant is the ancient myth of Hylas mentioned in Virgil, Eclogue 6.2.44–43: "His adiungit, Hylan nautae quo fonte relictum/clamassent, ut litus 'Hyla, Hyla' omne sonaret." ("To these he adds the story of the spring where Hylas was left and how the seamen called on him, till all the shore rang 'Hylas! Hylas!' ") In Greek mythology, Heracles spared Hylas the young son of King Theiodamas, whom he had defeated and killed. After making Hylas his page, they traveled together on the voyage of the Argonauts till landing at Cios. There Hylas went to fetch water, found a spring, and was pulled into the water by nymphs, who were in love with his beauty. Heracles stayed to look for him and this became the basis in Cios for a ritual search for Hylas.

29. *Oven Bird:* A warbler, whose call sounds like "preacher, preacher" or "teacher, teacher," that builds his domelike nest on the ground. See also the discussion of the oven bird (genus *Furnarius*) in Darwin's *The Voyage of the Beagle,* chapter 5, "Bahia Blanca."

30. *shed crystal . . . had fallen:* See Shelley's "Adonais," 52.462–64: "Life, like a dome of many-coloured glass,/Stains the white radiance of Eternity,/Until Death tramples it to fragments."

31. *orchid Calypso:* A bog herb named after the nymph Calypso, a goddess of silence who reigned on the island of Ogygia and offered Odysseus eternal youth and life if he would cease wandering and stay with her forever.

32. *"Out, Out":* Shakespeare, *Macbeth,* 5.5.23—"Out, out, brief candle!"—from Macbeth's speech on the death of his wife.

33. *Racker Sect:* Frost invented this name.

34. *Chickadee:* Titmouse, a small bird with thick plumage and a short bill.

35. *the gift of . . . tongues:* See Acts 2:4. The outpouring of spirit that enabled the Apostles to communicate in all foreign languages.

36. *Stone-Boat:* A low, flat sled used for transporting stones.

37. *Bird of Paradise's tail:* The Bird of Paradise is a tropical bird prized for its brilliantly colored plumes.

38. *Wave offering:* An offering waved before the Lord; for example, in Numbers 5, 6, 18, and 20; Leviticus 7, 8, 9, 10, 14, and 23; Exodus 29.

39. *Wild Grapes:* Isaiah 5:2—"And he fenced it, and gathered out the stones thereof, and planted it with the choicest vine, and built a tower in the midst of it, and also made a winepress therein: and he looked that it should bring forth grapes and it brought forth wild grapes."

40. *What tree . . . birch:* Cf. Matthew 7:16—"Ye shall know them by their fruits. Do men gather grapes of thorns, or figs of thistles?"

41. *Eurydice:* In classical mythology, Orpheus attempts to rescue Eurydice from the underworld but is ordered not to look back at her while leading her out of Hades. He turns toward her when they come into sight of the upper regions, and she disappears.

42. *Leif . . . German:* Leif Ericsson (fl. A.D. 1000), an Icelandic explorer who was driven off course and by luck became the first known discoverer of a land rich in self-cultivating wheat, timber, and grapes that he called "Vinland," or "Wineland, the Good," in North America, possibly some part of Nova Scotia. He carried specimens of wild, grape-bearing vines back to Greenland. Although

there is no contemporaneous record of his discovery, it is supported by Adam of Bremen (Germany) in *Gesta Hammaburgenis Ecclesiae Pontificum* (1595).

43. *COÖS:* Coos County in northern New Hampshire.

44. *the Sioux Control:* A U.S. agent in charge of the affairs of the Sioux Indian tribe. Here he acts as a spiritualist.

45. *The Wild Colonial Boy:* Australian folk song.

46. *GRAFTON:* County in central New Hampshire.

47. *Rogers' Rangers:* Rangers commanded by Robert Rogers (1731–95) in the Seven Years' War (1756–63).

48. *E. T. . . . poems:* British essayist Edward Thomas (1878–1917) became a close friend of Frost's and began writing poetry soon after. He joined the army in 1915, and after his death in 1917, Frost succeeded in having a collection of Thomas's poems published in America.

49. *Vimy Ridge:* Captured by Canadian and British troops, April 9–10, 1917, during the Battle of Arras. Thomas was serving with the Royal Garrison Artillery and was killed by a German shell on April 9, several miles south of the ridge.

50. *Truth? A pebble of quartz?:* It was a saying of ancient Greek philosophy that truth could be found at the bottom of a well.

INDEX OF TITLES
AND FIRST LINES

A governor it was proclaimed this time,   98
A house that lacks, seemingly, mistress and master,   18
A lantern light from deeper in the barn   117
A neighbor of mine in the village   173
A plow, I hear men say, to plow the snow   260
A saturated meadow,   17
A stranger came to the door at eve,   7
After Apple-Picking   92
Aim Was Song, The   248
All crying, "We will go with you, O Wind!"   257
All out of doors looked darkly in at him   141
Always the same, when on a fated night   251
As I went down the hill along the wall   153
Asking for Roses   18
Ax-Helve, The   217

Before man came to blow it right   248
Birches   157
Black Cottage, The   78
Blueberries   82
Blue-Butterfly Day   250
Bond and Free   156
Bonfire, The   169
BOY'S WILL, A   1
Brook in the City, A   254
Brown lived at such a lofty farm   179
Brown's Descent   179
By June our brook's run out of song and speed   154

Census-Taker, The   208
Christmas Trees   138

Code, The   94
Come with rain, O loud Southwester!   14
Cow in Apple Time, The   162

Death of the Hired Man, The   53
Demiurge's Laugh, The   38
Dream Pang, A   21
Dust of Snow   246

Encounter, An   163
Even the bravest that are slain   27
Evening in a Sugar Orchard   255
Exposed Nest, The   175
Fear, The   117
Fire and Ice   245
Flower-Gathering   16
For Once, Then, Something   249
From where I lingered in a lull of March   255

Generations of Men, The   98
Ghost House   4
Girl's Garden, A   173
Going for Water   25
Good Hours   134
Good-by and Keep Cold   252
Grindstone, The   221
Gum-Gatherer, The   182

Having a wheel and four legs of its own   221
He is said to have been the Last Red Man   185
He saw her from the bottom of the stairs   73
Her teacher's certainty it must be Mabel   210
Here come the line-gang pioneering by   184
Hill Wife, The   165
Hillside Thaw, A   258
Home Burial   73
Housekeeper, The   107
How countlessly they congregate   10
Hundred Collars, A   65
Hyla Brook   154

I came an errand one cloud-blowing evening   208
I didn't make you know how glad I was   86
I dwell in a lonely house I know   4
I had for my winter evening walk—   134
I had withdrawn in forest, and my song   21
I left you in the morning,   16
I let myself in at the kitchen door   107
I slumbered with your poems on my breast   247
I stayed the night for shelter at a farm   236
I walked down alone Sunday after church   159
I went to turn the grass once after one   32
I wonder about the trees   202
If tired of trees I seek again mankind,   23
In a Vale   20
In Equal Sacrifice   30
In Neglect   22
In the Home Stretch   143
Into My Own   3
It is blue-butterfly day here in spring,   250
It was far in the sameness of the wood;   38
It went many years,   262
I'm going out to clean the pasture spring;   49
I've known ere now an interfering branch   217

Lancaster bore him—such a little town,   65
Late Walk, A   9
Line-Gang, The   184
Line-Storm Song, A   40
Lockless Door, The   262
Love and a Question   7
Love has earth to which she clings   156
Lovers, forget your love,   12

Maple   210
Mary sat musing on the lamp-flame at the table   53
Meeting and Passing   153
Mending Wall   51
Misgiving   257
MOUNTAIN INTERVAL   135
Mountain, The   60
Mowing   24

My Butterfly   43
My long two-pointed ladder's sticking through a tree   92
My November Guest   6
My Sorrow, when she's here with me   6

Need of Being Versed in Country Things, The   263
Never tell me that not one star of all   205
NORTH OF BOSTON   47
Not to Keep   253
Nothing to say to all those marriages!   233
Now close the windows and hush all the fields;   39
Now Close the Windows   39

O hushed October morning mild,   42
October   42
Oh, give us pleasure in the flowers today;   15
"Oh, let's go up the hill and scare ourselves,   169
Old Man's Winter Night, An   141
On a Tree Fallen Across the Road   261
Once on the kind of day called "weather breeder,"   163
One of my wishes is that those dark trees,   3
One ought not to have to care   165
Onset, The   251
Others taunt me with having knelt at well-curbs   249
"Out, Out—"   177
Out through the fields and the woods   45
Out walking in the frozen swamp one grey day   132
Oven Bird, The   155

Pan came out of the woods one day,—   36
Pan with Us   36
Pasture, The   49
Patch of Old Snow, A   142
Paul's Wife   224
Pea Brush   159
Place for a Third   233
Plowmen   260
Prayer in Spring, A   15
Putting in the Seed   160

Range-Finding   164
Reluctance   45
Revelation   26
Road Not Taken, The   137
Rose Pogonias   17

Self-Seeker, The   122
Servant to Servants, A   86
She stood against the kitchen sink, and looked   143
Snow   186
Some say the world will end in fire,   245
Something inspires the only cow of late   162
Something there is that doesn't love a wall,   51
Sound of the Trees, The   202
Spoils of the Dead   34
Star in a Stone-Boat, A   205
Stars   10
Storm Fear   11

Telephone, The   152
The battle rent a cobweb diamond-strung   164
The buzz-saw snarled and rattled in the yard   177
The city had withdrawn into itself   138
The farmhouse lingers, though averse to square   254
The house had gone to bring again   263
The line-storm clouds fly tattered and swift,   40
The mountain held the town as in a shadow   60
The sound of the closing outside door was all   256
The three stood listening to a fresh access   186
The tree the tempest with a crash of wood   261
The way a crow   246
The well was dry beside the door,   25
There is a singer everyone has heard,   155
There overtook me and drew me in   182
There was never a sound beside the wood but one,   24
There were three in the meadow by the brook   94
There's a patch of old snow in a corner   142
They leave us so to the way we took,   22
They sent him back to her. The letter came   253
Thine emulous fond flowers are dead, too,   43
This saying good-by on the edge of the dark   252

Thus of old the Douglas did: 30
Time to Talk, A   161
To drive Paul out of any lumber camp   224
To E. T.   247
To the Thawing Wind   14
To think to know the country and not know   258
Trial by Existence, The   27
Tuft of Flowers, The   32
Two fairies it was   34
Two roads diverged in a yellow wood,   137
Two Witches   236

Valley's Singing Day, The   256
Vanishing Red, The   185
Vantage Point, The   23

Waiting   19
We chanced in passing by that afternoon   78
We make ourselves a place apart   26
What things for dream there are when spectre-like,   19
What tree may not the fig be gathered from?   229
When a friend calls to me from the road   161
When I go up through the mowing field,   9
When I see birches bend to left and right   157
"When I was just as far as I could walk   152
When I was young, we dwelt in a vale   20
When the wind works against us in the dark,   11
Wild Grapes   229
"Willis, I didn't want you here today: 122
Wind and Window Flower   12
Wood-Pile, The   132

You come to fetch me from my work to-night   160
"You ought to have seen what I saw on my way   82
You were forever finding some new play   175